Reset Your Mind, Body and Spirit

Mandeep S. Jalota is an Indian Revenue Service (IRS) officer of the 2013 batch who is currently serving as the Joint Commissioner of GST, Mumbai. He graduated with a degree in computer sciences.

Mandeep has struggled with depression and anxiety for much of his life, but he successfully managed to come out of it on his own. Since then, he has been dedicating his time to helping people who struggle with depression, anxiety, obsessive–compulsive disorder and other mental health issues.

Through his writing, the author hopes to help others break free from the darkness of depression and anxiety, find courage and heal. His book is a valuable resource for anyone struggling with depression.

Reset Your Mind, Body and Spirit

A Survivor's Guide to Overcoming **ANXIETY** and **DEPRESSION**

MANDEEP S. JALOTA

RUPA

Published by
Rupa Publications India Pvt. Ltd 2023
7/16, Ansari Road, Daryaganj
New Delhi 110002

Copyright © Mandeep S. Jalota 2023
Illustrations courtesy: Mandeep S. Jalota

The views and opinions expressed in this book are the author's own and
the facts are as reported by him which have been verified to the extent
possible, and the publishers are not in any way liable for the same.

P-ISBN: 978-93-5702-537-9
E-ISBN: 978-93-5702-538-6

Fifth impression 2024

10 9 8 7 6 5

The moral right of the author has been asserted.

Contents

1

Introduction

This book is for people like me who get stressed because of life's everyday uncertainties, for those who helplessly see themselves in a never-ending spiral, where stress leads to anxiety and anxiety leads to depression and depression leads to a life that feels meaningless. This book is for those who can't figure out why life is so messy without any particular reason and why we often feel emotionally drained, lethargic, lose interest in what we are doing or why our mind is obsessively fixated on certain things.

I have suffered from depression and general anxiety disorder for years. Every doctor, every medicine and every method failed to cure me. I had reached a point where I was unable to imagine a life where I could ever feel happy. I also reconciled myself to remain an underachiever professionally. That's when I decided to take the help of my real enemy—my mind—to vanquish anxiety and depression. It's taken me five years, but now I know the method to defeat them each time.

I believe that being happy is the main aim of our life—to live and experience the beautiful gift of life—which most of us seek from external sources. Yes, happiness does exist in the external world, but it also comes from within. Being wealthy and resourceful may not ensure being in a happy state. The world is full of complexities and differences. While it may not be in our hands where we are born (some of us may have to work hard to earn a meagre sum whereas others are born rich and may not need to earn anything in their life), one thing is for sure—everyone deserves to be happy so that they can experience life in a vibrant way.

But, as it often happens, we are drained of energy or prone to trauma; hold grudges against one and all; struggle with our sense of self; are unable to use our potential and talent; are unable to give due importance to our studies, our personal life and our professional life because of the above-mentioned problems. I too lived like this for many years because there was no one to guide me or pull me out of this mess.

When I went through hardships and witnessed others closely who were similarly troubled, I learnt many lessons, which I hope will be of help to others. I never came across any text that not only discusses the concept of understanding yourself clearly but also provides a practical guide to dealing with matters of the mind. This book is thus a result of applying all the approaches that I came across while attempting to heal myself and I'll be sharing those that actually work.

Now, the first thing that we need to focus on is our brain. In its quest for self-exploration, the human brain has evolved over the ages. Today, it is considered a wonder of nature that has dealt with drastic changes in civilization, particularly in the modern motorized and information age. (*Goli maar bheje mein* [...] *Ke bheja shor karta hai.*) No, I don't recommend you shoot your brain, as written by Gulzar for the 1998 Bollywood flick *Satya's* soundtrack. Rather, we need to first understand certain basics pertaining to our brain, because then only we will be able to keep it healthy and mobilize it to achieve success, good health and good fortune, thereby making life stable and hassle-free. There are many people around us who are silently suffering—emotionally abusing themselves and others without realizing that they are the cause of their own and others' suffering.

In this book, I explain how we can hold a mirror to our minds. We can be aware of our mind's mechanics and get greater insights into the thought processes behind our actions. I specifically focus on the general issues, whether they are experiences, prejudices, biases or lopsided thinking, irrespective of the strata, situation, place and time.

As we have no working manual for the mind, I explore various ways to understand how the mind works and why our mind takes us for a ride while we think we are the master. I also discuss how we can train our brain so that it doesn't use us against ourselves, whether by convincing us to seek pleasure in harmful habits or making us think about our negative experiences in an unending loop. Our brain often dampens our ability to find out ways to overcome depression and makes us behave obsessively without trusting anyone.

The second thing that is closely associated with the mind and matters the most is a well-rested mind. Having a good night's sleep is as essential as oxygen is for our survival. I have suggested a few ways by which we can regulate our sleep for a healthier mind. This is followed by dietary changes that enable us to improve our gut health because a healthy gut also results in a healthy brain. In recent ground-breaking research, a possible connection has been revealed between our gut microbiome, eating habits and the onset of Alzheimer's disease.[1]

---

[1]Cammann, Davis, Yimei Lu, Melika J. Cummings, Mark L. Zhang, Joan Manuel Cue, Jenifer Do, Jeffrey Ebersole, Xiangning Chen, Edwin C. Oh, Jeffrey L. Cummings, and Jingchun Chen, 'Genetic Correlations between Alzheimer's Disease and Gut Microbiome Genera', *Scientific Reports*, Vol. 13, 2023, 5258. https://doi.org/10.1038/s41598-023-31730-5. Accessed on 22 May 2023.

The other things that I believe are also important are as follows: including physical exercises as an integral part of our life to bid goodbye to our usually sedentary lifestyle, developing a habit of diary-writing to reinforce positivity, reconnecting with our spirit(uality) and so on. Thus, I present to you workable solutions in this book for balancing your mind, body and spirit, which I further expand on in each chapter.

I consider all the above with examples that I gathered from my experiences, observations, stories that are already known worldwide and motivational anecdotes that I came across in my life as well as other sources (whether it be the internet, newspaper articles or books such as *The Body: A Guide for Occupants* by Bill Bryson and *The Upward Spiral: Using Neuroscience to Reverse the Course of Depression, One Small Change at a Time* by Alex Korb). I have meticulously presented all these materials, which will force you to take a pause, attach it to your experiences and understand your past and present events in order to make positive future plans.

I have attempted to simplify everything so that my learnings can easily be applied by anyone to their lives. This book is for readers from all walks of life, whether they are young or a hundred years old, especially those who are willing to introspect their past and present lives; the basic principles remain almost the same. This is equally a guide for those who feel they are successful but not satisfied, are suffering from adolescent issues or a mid-life crisis and even for those leading an unhappy retired life.

But, I must emphasize that the views presented in this book are personal and thus, they may not be helpful for everyone. It is not meant to be a substitute for professional and medical help; I advise you to use your wisdom. It is not a clinical diagnostic instrument, but it should help you in figuring out and ameliorating symptoms of stress, anxiety, depression, phobias, obsessive–compulsive disorder (OCD) and various mental ailments. If you have any concerns, I implore you to consult medical professionals. If a family member is experiencing similar issues, you can help them by suggesting the ideas presented in this book so that they may have a chance to improve their mental and general health.

There are ample things that are unknown to man. This book is for those too who are looking for evidence-based treatment for mental issues. It is from the perspective of a patient who remains under-represented most of the time. This book is not only for people who are struggling with anxiety, depression and OCD but also for people who want to learn more about these concepts. It answers a lot of questions that usually crop up in our minds. So, let's give up useless and ineffective ways to dismantle our mental barriers and forever change our life for good by resetting our mind, body and spirit.

I urge you all to take this irreversible step to reclaim your life.

◆

UNDERSTANDING OUR BRAIN

As we delve deeper into the intricacies of the brain,
we begin to unlock the secrets of the mind and the
mysteries of human behaviour.

—Anonymous

Depression is generally perceived by us as a state of being constantly sad, though the condition is far deeper than that. There is a constant sense of low energy, hollowness or insecurity; inability to concentrate and take any decisions; emotional numbness; the compulsion to think in a negative way; and feelings of guilt and obsession about things, issues and people. Depression may consist of a combination of some or all of these symptoms. It affects you physically like having pain in the body or a feeling of being sick, as if you are having a cardiac arrest or an acid reflux. It can also result in being prone to phobias and manias and becoming suspicious of other people's activities. The symptoms change for each individual.

In day-to-day conversation, we casually use the word 'depression' as a synonym for sadness. But in medical terminology, it's a state that lasts longer than an immediate feeling of sadness. It is a state when we cannot return to normalcy even after a considerable time lapse; in fact, we can go even deeper.

When you stay in survival mode (which is the term I use to refer to people with depression), you are not able to focus on your profession and personal life because you are consciously and subconsciously focussing on maintaining the normal functions of the body. When it becomes a daily occurrence and you start facing difficulty in initiating new things, that's an alarm bell warning you that your mind is not on the right track because somewhere, it is fighting underlying depression or some other mental ailment, leading to a shutdown of activities in those parts of the brain that allow us to initiate new things. For instance, it may become difficult to get out of bed, get assignments done, do your office work, etc. On the contrary, you wish to run away from work every time. These are not normal symptoms that we can ignore when we make excessive excuses in trying to justify not working. Everyone has depressive tendencies to varying degrees, but some bounce back to normal life and some don't. Those who bounce back may still be having traces of depression, which lower their quality of life. However, they may not be diagnosed as clinically depressed. In the last few decades, medical science has seen various advances in understanding the functioning of the brain, but there is still a lot more research to be done.

Thus, in this section, we are going to paint a picture of the brain in a simplistic way. There may be quite a few technical terms but don't get overwhelmed by them. I suggest you keep reading even if you can't fully grasp the meaning of the text in front of you.

◆

By the 1960s, depression and other ailments were considered to be caused due to the deficiency/imbalance of neurotransmitters (chemical messengers or molecules used by the nervous system to transmit messages between neurons, or from neurons to muscles).

While most diseases are defined by their causes, depression is defined and diagnosed by a set of symptoms—not being able to take decisions, getting irritated, etc. No magnetic resonance imaging (MRI), electroencephalography (EEG) or any other sort of brain scan can diagnose depression.

The Diagnostic and Statistical Manual of Mental Disorders urges medical professionals to consider the diagnosis of depression when someone goes through a trauma, such as the death of a near or dear one, facing a breakup or loss of a job, feeling constantly insecure or having a persistent or terminal disease. The advice is to wait for at least two months as it is natural to feel depressive under the above-mentioned circumstances. However, if the person does not return to a normal state after the aforementioned period, then a particular neurological treatment may be taken up.

Our brain is a complex system that has ultimate control over the body. The brain operates via neurotransmitters, the prefrontal cortex, the limbic system and the spinal cord. **Neurotransmitters** are chemical messengers that transmit signals from nerve cells to target cells. Their functioning will provide you with a new perspective to see your mental well-being in terms of these neurochemicals because each happy chemical triggers a different feeling.

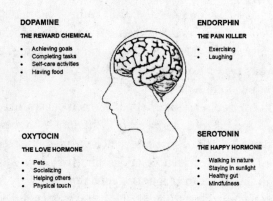

**HAPPINESS CHEMICALS AND
HOW TO HACK THEM**

DOPAMINE

THE REWARD CHEMICAL

- Achieving goals
- Completing tasks
- Self-care activities
- Having food

ENDORPHIN

THE PAIN KILLER

- Exercising
- Laughing

OXYTOCIN

THE LOVE HORMONE

- Pets
- Socializing
- Helping others
- Physical touch

SEROTONIN

THE HAPPY HORMONE

- Walking in nature
- Staying in sunlight
- Healthy gut
- Mindfulness

Serotonin, also known as the 'happy hormone', works as a mood stabilizer, which in turn initiates feelings of well-being, contentment and happiness. It enables brain cells and other cells of the nervous system to communicate with each other. It is also the reason behind having good sleep, a hearty appetite, proper digestion, relaxation and being happy.

This is followed by **oxytocin**, which is also called the 'cuddle hormone' or 'feel-good hormone'. Oxytocin is produced by the hypothalamus and released by the pituitary gland when we're physically affectionate, producing what may be described as feelings of connection, bonding and trust.

A mother's love for her children is generated because of oxytocin. It increases feelings of trust and security and bonding and alleviates fear and anxiety. It also increases when we interact socially. When there is less oxytocin, we feel withdrawn and isolated. Mothers, who find it easy to abandon their children, probably do so because of a shortage of oxytocin.

Next up are **endorphins**, which are natural pain relievers and also stimulate pleasure. These are produced, for example, when you're pushing your body to the limit while exercising.

Another neurochemical is **dopamine**, which is the reason behind the feeling of joy when you find something that you were seeking—the 'Eureka! I got it!' moment. It is triggered even when you wake up early and clean the house, arrange books, change the bed sheets or clean the floor; the sense of achievement that you experience after finishing the tasks you set out to do is because of dopamine.

But when dopamine is in excess, it may lead you to behave like (say) Alexander the Great (which is obviously harmful since you have started losing your grip on reality). Conversely, a shortage of dopamine can result in Parkinson's disease.

◆

The brain consists of the prefrontal cortex, limbic system and spinal cord.

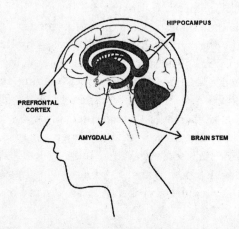

The **logical mind**, or the **prefrontal cortex**, performs the functions of reasoning, problem-solving, comprehension, impulse control and creativity. It has gradually evolved, at different times, with the evolution of humans. As humans, we have the most developed prefrontal cortex when compared with animals. Rather, it is what makes us human.

The **limbic system** controls our behavioural and **emotional responses** (especially when it comes to behaviours that we need for survival, such as feeding, reproduction and fight-or-flight responses). This system was introduced in 1952 by American neuroscientist Paul MacLean, and it mainly includes the hippocampus, amygdala and hypothalamus.

About the size of a peanut, the **hypothalamus** controls the chemistry of the body, regulates hunger and monitors blood sugar, sleep and sexual functions. Taken from the Greek word for 'seahorse', the **hippocampus** plays a nodal role in **etching memories in the brain**. It is closely related to depression and decreases in size when you are more depressed. Greek for 'almond', the **amygdala** handles intense and **stressful**

emotions, such as anxiety, phobia, anger and fear.

The 'bus system' of neurons, the **spinal cord**, starts from the lower part of the brain and extends to the lower back; the oldest part of the brain, called the brain stem, is an integral part of it. Its major functions are electrochemical communication, walking and reflexes. It is the most primitive part of the body from where our brain originated and started growing.

Two parts of the brain that are involved in mental ailments, especially depression, are the prefrontal cortex and the limbic system. The prefrontal cortex is involved in logical and rational thinking, whereas the limbic system concerns itself with feelings and emotions.

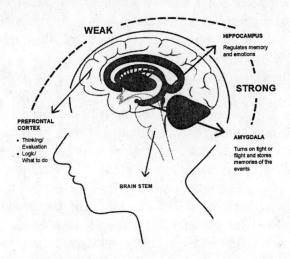

Due to less production/retention of serotonin, the prefrontal cortex (the logical mind) may become weak, and the limbic part (emotional brain) starts taking over the reins of the entire brain system. Just a little trigger of negative events can make our prefrontal cortex (logical reasoning) easily hand over control to the emotional brain, resulting in a decline in our logical reasoning and triggering the fight-or-flight response (i.e. automatic physiological reaction to events that are perceived as stressful or frightening).

Some patients attribute their mental ailments to their genes. What's the role of genes? Can we change them? Our genes are inherited and include certain information that may, in future generations, lead to depression. We can say that genes are like loaded guns, where the trigger lies in how you manage your body and mind, along with your surroundings. Self-knowledge about the mind and body is the most important factor for staying fit. I have often come across people who are so complacent about their unhealthy lifestyle that they have no will to change it. Instead, they blame their genes and other factors in the environment. They seem to hold their unhealthy lifestyles dearer than life itself.

For example, if an accident occurs in a city on a busy route, it may lead to traffic resulting from roadblocks for hours. Just a single casualty can cause trouble for the general public and traffic police. Similarly, but on a more complex level, the brain, as designed by nature, has billions of neurons and circuits containing memories, which communicate with each other, making it possible to have life in the body. Say, there is a short circuit in the communication of neurons, which leads to no signal or faulty signal. Mismanagement because of our lifestyle, traumas, unbalanced diets, lopsided thinking and so on may place the whole brain system into chaos and lead to a gradual shutting down of various activities and processes for the brain to save its resources and bounce back to normalcy. Most of us don't realize the basic requirements of the body, which include how we think and feel, the importance of sleeping on time, exercising, not getting into the loop of negative thought processes and having a proper diet, thus moving slowly towards silent trauma.

But the good news is that today, we can modify our brain circuits and balance the level of neurochemicals and grow new brain cells not only by medication but also by changing our thought processes and lifestyles. Small variations in our lifestyle and thinking habits can have a huge impact on mental health as brain chemistry begins to change from a weaker to a robust state.

THE FIGHT-OR-FLIGHT RESPONSE

It's an automatic physiological (bodily) reaction to an event that is perceived as stressful or frightening. Say, in a primitive setting, you live in a jungle, and a ferocious animal runs after you. How will your body react? Now think about the same in a modern situation. You're stuck in traffic, and someone is honking at you. What will be your body's reaction then? Either you will fight with that person or take flight/ignore the situation.

How does the fight-or-flight response manifest itself?

When the fight-or-flight response is triggered, feelings of sympathy develop in the nervous system. The hippocampus stores negative experiences as memories and analyses threats in terms of people's past experiences. When faced with imminent threat, the hippocampus sends out alerts to other parts of the brain, and the amygdala (emotional brain) gets activated and releases cortisol and catecholamines (a class of aromatic amines that includes a number of neurotransmitters, such as adrenaline and dopamine) because the prefrontal cortex (the logical decision-maker) is unable to make the right judgement. So, the sympathetic nervous system (SNS) comes into play, the heart rate increases, blood pressure rises, there is rapid breathing, the mind becomes more focussed to react and the body is ready for the fight-or-flight response.

As the heart rate and blood pressure increase, the blood supply to the intestines gets reduced because blood is directed towards the legs and muscles so that physical activity can be performed in order to escape any sort of danger.

In a normal scenario, it is the parasympathetic nervous system (PNS, i.e. the relaxed state of the body and brain) that is functioning. So, when someone has anxiety issues, their fight-or-flight response (SNS) gets more active than their relaxed state (PNS).

Now you know that if your SNS gets triggered frequently, you have anxiety. You may have serious issues when your logical mind easily hands over the reins to the emotional brain, thus making you too emotionally reactive in day-to-day situations. So in case of mood swings or depression, what you may actually be having is an issue with serotonin production/retention in your body, similar to why you feel good after cuddling or exercising, and so on.

◆

Now that we are aware of how the most complex organ—our brain—works, let us have a look behind the scenes at how our mind, body and spirit are connected and allow this survivor to show you ways to reset them in order to overcome anxiety and depression.

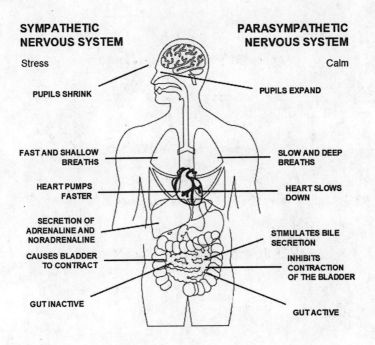

SYMPATHETIC NERVOUS SYSTEM

Stress

PUPILS SHRINK

FAST AND SHALLOW BREATHS

HEART PUMPS FASTER

SECRETION OF ADRENALINE AND NORADRENALINE

CAUSES BLADDER TO CONTRACT

GUT INACTIVE

PARASYMPATHETIC NERVOUS SYSTEM

Calm

PUPILS EXPAND

SLOW AND DEEP BREATHS

HEART SLOWS DOWN

STIMULATES BILE SECRETION

INHIBITS CONTRACTION OF THE BLADDER

GUT ACTIVE

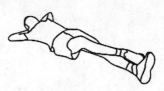

Sympathetic Response System

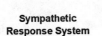

Fight or flight

Parasympathetic Response System

Rest and digest

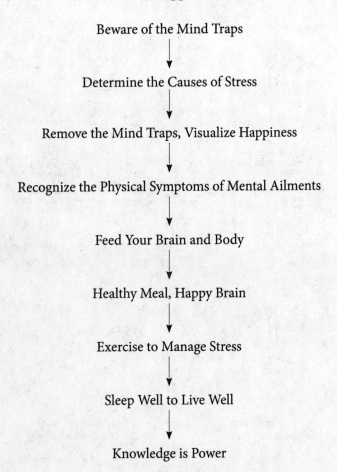

Crux of Your Happiness Journey

Beware of the Mind Traps

Determine the Causes of Stress

Remove the Mind Traps, Visualize Happiness

Recognize the Physical Symptoms of Mental Ailments

Feed Your Brain and Body

Healthy Meal, Happy Brain

Exercise to Manage Stress

Sleep Well to Live Well

Knowledge is Power

2

The Battle of Knowns and Unknowns

I've had a lot of worries in my life,
most of which never happened.

—Mark Twain

Heaven and hell are in your mind. If you are anxious and fearful and find yourself constantly reinforcing, albeit unknowingly, such negativity, you are creating your hell. It's as simple as that. Dis-ease is when you are uneasy with yourself. To switch on heaven mode, you need to change your frequency in this battle of knowns and unknowns. You are only as safe as your thoughts because you are constantly making neural networks, which may play a horror movie or a pleasant movie on auto mode.

We will start by understanding the basic principles of the mind that govern our happiness and unhappiness; when we are ignorant of ourselves, we attract mental and bodily ailments either immediately or in the long term. If we know more about ourselves, we will have a good quality of life. Our thought process is bound by certain unsaid traps and cheat codes, which we will learn in the following pages.

One of the differences between man and all other animals is that they have more options to get stressed out about, to be anxious and overthink because of their imagination. Our mental constructs, which we form through our experiences and facts and inferences, that help us in thinking, judging, prejudging and taking decisions, may also backfire if we don't realize how our brain works. What if there are unknown memories, fears, uncertainties and anxieties that you have been fighting, resenting or struggling with for years? Have you identified them? If yes, then you're doing great. If not, you can try to identify your mind's traps, which have imprisoned you for a long time.

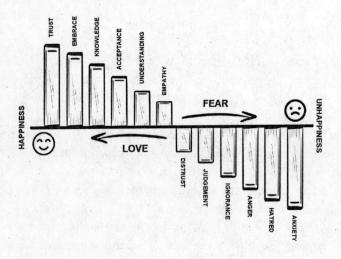

RECOGNIZE YOUR MIND TRAPS

Identifying the problem is the first step towards healing, and then comes acceptance. But sometimes, the psychological problem behaves like a chameleon. It remains hidden in the guise of a trap of emotional reactions, attachments and insecurities.

Trap 1: Negative Memories

Suffering is not holding you,
you are holding onto suffering.

—Osho

The mind is largely a prisoner of experiences and inferences it has drawn over a period of time. If our experiences have been bad due to certain reasons, then the probability of our thought processes getting corrupted becomes high. It is not surprising that our mind tends to mostly remember negative events because of the inherent survival instinct in order to save itself from any perceived threat. This is how nature has designed our minds.

Memory is a double-edged sword. If you remember more negative things from your past, then it is a problem and may create trouble in the present and surely bring down your future quality of life. For instance, someone who boasts of having a very sharp memory but only remembers every negative event from the past will keep on weaving their life around past negative experiences and refresh them frequently. A woman who says to her husband, 'I still remember what you said to my brother 20 years ago,' and goes on to relate every detail and then picks up a fight is not exhibiting a healthy sign.

We are not taught how to operate our minds when we are young and we generally tend to interpret people and situations according to our past experiences. So, chances are high that we keep piling up the negativities as we grow in age. It's like a mother who has a distorted view of things like passing on suspicions, insecurities and other negative viewpoints to her child.

It's hard to make most people understand that they can fall prey to the 'Fallacy of Practicality', meaning that they sustain the way they have experienced the world. The experiences they have gathered over their lifetime become a prominent part of their identity and personality and they are unable to think of their existence without these negative experiences, which they call 'being practical'. It's hard to convince such people to change and even when you explain the positive side of an issue, they will reject your point of view as being impractical and consider you as being over-optimistic. This fallacy of being practical actually becomes a hurdle in changing and broadening viewpoints.

◆

You may think you are suffering because of the past or what lies ahead in the future, but actually, you are suffering because of your memory and imagination. Holding on to past negative memories is like driving a car with breaks on, or an athlete carrying weights and running—this way you cannot enjoy the pleasures of driving or running.

Take the case of an old person, Pritam, who had a severe fear of snakes, which started intensifying as he grew older. The self-repetitions and self-affirmations in his mind made the negative cognitive component so strong that during the last days of his life, his mind was totally engulfed in the fear of snakes that he imagined would appear out of thin air and bite him. Actually, no snake ever bit him!

A friend of mine was in love with a girl, but both of their families were against the idea of the two getting married. As a result, the girl was married off to someone else. Soon, he started imagining that his family members were conspiring against him. Even today (12-13 years later), when we call him during winter time, the period when the girl was married, we find him usually admitted to a psychiatric hospital when his suspicion level against his family increases. He develops symptoms or a mental imbalance and stays in the hospital for 1-2 months before returning. This is how his subconscious is working against him.

Take another case, that of Arun, whose father died of a heart attack a few years ago. Soon, his father's brother also developed cardiac issues and an angioplasty was performed. Now, Arun started feeling pain around his chest frequently. This scared him as he could not help but think that there was a heart condition that ran in his family. The more he thought, the stronger the negativity became. One day he had a strong pain in his chest for which he was admitted to a hospital and after all the tests were conducted, he was found to be absolutely fine. After he was given stress-relieving tablets, he showed improvement. Today, Arun is fine.

◆

In my office, a retired officer of my department met with me over some issues. Soon, we were chatting informally and he told me about his last days before retirement. He told me that he would have been a chief commissioner still in service had some senior officer not threatened him with a vigilance case. Since he would risk losing his gratuity and other benefits, he had to take voluntary retirement. I could see the resentment in his eyes, the grief over whatever happened and the emotional pain of not retiring as chief commissioner. It was truly making him sick.

Anita, who recently got married to a boy in Australia, was being haunted by her ex, who was living in India. She had always been under the impression that her ex may try to harm her parents back in India, and this was affecting her mental health. She wasn't getting proper sleep, which was making her condition worse. However, as part of an exercise, she was told that it wasn't the boy but the mental construct of that boy in her mind that was disturbing her. She was subsequently advised to change the construct of her ex-boyfriend since it's usually very difficult to control the mind as negative thoughts tend to cling and don't leave easily. Changing the construct of the ex would help her bring about a positive change in her emotions. This small exercise gave her much relief. (We will learn more about this technique subsequently.)

◆

There is another example of a girl who appeared for the civil services exam three times but could not get the job or appear again as the attempts were limited to three. The constant regret that she could have done better was haunting her consciously and subconsciously and became the source of her pain, but she could not get rid of this and started believing that she was unlucky, thus lowering her self-esteem, which wreaked havoc on her body and mind. Like this girl, we too don't usually realize that holding on to such memories can hugely impact our worldview. We see everything through regret and negative perspectives, which degrades the quality of our life.

A young man, who was traumatized from being rejected in love, internalized his feelings of anger, resentment and rejection to the extent that he would hurl abuses at cars in front of him, asking the car owners to move their cars that were, in fact, parked on the side of the road. When he got down from his car, he would often see no one inside the other car. Such a person can be said to be in conflict with the system itself, similar to those who keep posting complaint letters to various departments over petty issues. Such people are holding a burning coal in their hands to throw at someone when actually, they are only hurting themselves.

◆

Many people hold on to grudges, and when they can't take revenge on a more powerful person, they target other innocent people in their personal or professional lives. For example, there are many who come into conflict with the system. They have learned all kinds of loopholes in the law, rules and regulations, and systematically start plotting, hatching and using their intellect to unnecessarily settle scores with everyone. The irony is that such people cannot differentiate between their negative instincts and intellect. Their intellect becomes a slave of these negative instincts and they start indulging in sadistic activities.

Trap 2: Guilt and Shame

If you have made a fortune by benefitting at the cost of weak people, the seed of this weed or guilt may engulf your mind in due course of time. Some people intentionally indulge in dishonest or unlawful acts to earn an easy name, fame or money, or other gains in life. They have inculcated bad emotions in their minds. This slow poison of guilt or insecurity remains in the subconscious mind and they grow gradually without knowledge if you don't introspect. The mind is like a garden; the feelings or seeds of guilt have been sown, and they grow as you grow older; you may consciously forget the events that have been wrongly done but the subconscious has gotten used to the pattern of bad feelings, such as guilt or resentment, which grow slowly and soon you start developing an uneasiness for which you find no specific reason, and this uneasiness may turn out to be a disease.

> The mind wants to perceive itself as good. It wants to be good in its eyes. Even when it has to do wrong, it will try to justify the wrong.

I have come across many older people who were once involved in anti-social activities and are now either highly religious or alcoholics to rid themselves of the guilt and insecurity they feel for wrongdoing; they frequently go to various temples, mosques, listen to bhajans, etc. to feel a sense of relief, while some excessively indulge in alcohol. (Not every person who goes to religious places is a 'sinner', of course.)

GUILT

I MADE A MISTAKE

Holding something we've done or failed to do up against our values and feeling psychological discomfort.

SHAME

I AM A MISTAKE

The intensely painful feeling or experience of believing that we are flawed and therefore unworthy of love and belonging.

People who are inflicted with a feeling of shame are not easily recognisable; also, it's difficult to differentiate between a depressed person and someone who has a feeling of deep-rooted shame in their personality. Such people live by their self-made standards or those inherited from their primary caregivers, such as their mothers. They have a severe feeling of insecurity about being rejected, so they don't get involved with other people and have almost no friends with whom they can share their secrets and emotions. This is because during their upbringing they have been told that they are intrinsically wrong rather than some specific task that has been wrongly performed. Children who are brought up like this start considering themselves to be wrong, deprecate themselves, have low confidence in life, do not open up in front of others and don't consider themselves worthy of love. It is a basic human need to accept ourselves along with limitations as none of us are perfect.

There are other kinds of memories that unconsciously pile up with time and one day, you start feeling depressed or anxious. For example, Radhika lost her mother six months ago, and has now started experiencing acid reflux and feeling low. She does not know the reason why it's happening but her past experiences along with the latest event of losing her mother have subconsciously left her in a chaotic state where she feels that something is wrong. This can be viewed under post-traumatic stress disorder (PTSD). But why is it wrong? She doesn't have an answer to that. The point is that all things get recorded in your mind. So, always remain vigilant and try to keep your mental records as clear as possible.

Trap 3: Uncertainty

When fear starts interfering with your freedom to live normally, then it's the start of a problem that may, over a period of time, become a major issue for you. You will always find something to be fearful about—what if the elevator breaks, what if the plane crashes, what if I go bankrupt, what will happen after retirement, what will happen if my children do not take care of me in old age, soon I am going to get some terrible disease or something may happen to my children and so on.

Such uncertainties are drawn from the belief system that has been formed through learning negative experiences from near and dear ones, from overthinking or from certain memories that may or may not be a part of the conscious mind but exist in the subconscious.

For example, my uncle does not like going out-of-station with his family or by himself, so whenever there is a situation where someone has to go for some important family work, he picks up a fight on some other issue out of insecurity and usually the plan gets cancelled. This happens due to the belief that he will be unable to manage things outside. What if something goes wrong? So, the cause is different but the outcome is a fight on some issue or the other. However, my uncle may not be aware of what he does. This is escapism or can be seen as creating drama to avoid situations.

In another example, parents may get over-possessive over their children, which may be because of their experiences in life. So, if a mother, who is always anxious about the whereabouts of her daughter, needs to hear everything that has happened in school, know her friends, etc., she unknowingly makes her daughter emotionally dependent on her to the extent that she leaves no space for her daughter to make friends. This way, the daughter's social circle gets reduced and that will actually cost her dearly later in life.

A person may have shifted to a distant place away from family or friends, away from their comfort zone; they feel lonely with an underlying fear or uncertainty that if something happens to them—whether financially, physically or emotionally—they will not be sure where to get support from. This underlying fear puts a huge pressure on them to the extent that they may leave their work/study in the new place and move back to their home where their comfort zone lies. Or it can lead to indulging in excessive drinking, smoking or other negative coping habits. This is commonly called nostalgia, but for some, it's so huge that they have to give up their jobs and return to their native place. Here are some suggestions on how to cope with changes in your workplace:

1. Before leaving for the new place of work, make an affirmation and visualize your work in a positive sense.

2. Try to collect information about the area and make your mind connect to that place. See the map of the city, feel comfortable with it and visualize it.

3. Try to find friends or connections within your community before going or immediately upon reaching the place. Find people with the same hobbies. Expand your circle as fast as possible.

4. Explore new places. The central idea is to make your mind comfortable.

5. Stay connected with your family on video calls.

6. Find a vehicle at your disposal, so that it can give you a sense of freedom that you can move anywhere whenever you want.

7. You must visit a doctor in case the situation gets unbearable.

Trap 4: Can't let it go

There was this person from a non-business background, who struggled, worked hard day and night and learnt all the trade secrets through his failures and successes. He then set up good manufacturing units in partnership with someone else. But when the business had thrived for some years, his partner duped him of crores of rupees. Despite this loss, he was able to retain his manufacturing plant. But the feeling of being deceived and resentment hit him hard, and soon, he started developing liver problems that couldn't be controlled. He constantly nagged about the complications he developed thinking of the partner who had betrayed him—a topic that would come up again and again in his conversations. Eventually, he died of medical complications at a young age. He was in his 40s.

This was an example of someone who didn't let go of the person who had harmed him, even though there was nothing he could do to change the situation. So, when you can't do much about the person you resent, for your sake, forgive them, otherwise the resentment and anger will forever burn within your mind and body. Remember, the person who deceived you has a similar mind to yours, so let his guilty feelings grow. Nature has its secret ways of working. Let nature do its work. Let the psychological karma work on them.

At times, there are some small issues that we ignore or fail to understand. For example, sometimes it is important to differentiate between professional life and personal life; otherwise, we may suffer from great misery. Bringing professional problems home and reacting rudely with the spouse or family members as you behave in the office strictly does not work. Both lives need a different set of norms. Also, problems in personal life are more difficult and can seriously impact professional life. In order to maintain balance and live harmoniously, we need to be emotionally intelligent; otherwise, marriage can be a hotbed of resentment, unhappiness and constant anger.

In contrast, it is better to let go of toxic relationships as they become a source of mental trouble, so much so that they can turn abusive, resulting in full-fledged oppression over a period of time. It is better to get out of it.

Working in an office in a dedicated manner is a responsibility but sometimes, obsession with office work not only disrupts your personal life, your spouse's and children's lives but also your staff's lives, especially those working under you. Being good at work is good, but sometimes expecting too much from the staff and policing them becomes an issue, causing frequent discord within the office. Some employees do have excessive issues with correcting the grammar of their juniors. In my previous job, one employee kept correcting his words again and again. This all happens due to underlying insecurity. This could be an obsessive–compulsive personality disorder trait.

Being honest is very commendable but boasting about it, judging, misjudging and prejudging others affect your relationships with others, which will surely affect your mind too.

Think about it: We must understand the fact that trust in relationships is required, but when we trust more than necessary, then we expose ourselves to getting duped, and when we trust less, then we invite mental ailments and sour relationships.

If you suspect your spouse too much, the relationship will suffer. Conversely, not caring enough about each other is also troublesome.

In the office, if you suspect all your juniors of taking a bribe or working with an ulterior motive, it will surely change your manner of addressing them, and the staff will also become hostile to your behaviour. However, while handling files, if you are not reading them properly and overly trusting your staff, you may land in trouble as well.

So, use your intellect to remain vigilant about balancing trust in your personal and professional life.

Suppose a child has grown up in a relative's family along with other children where his primary caregivers (parents) were missing. There's a huge probability that he will be bullied by other kids who know that he is an orphan, and the sense of unworthiness, trust problems and suspicions may start taking root both at the conscious and subconscious levels in the child. Even if the child is not being discriminated against by the elders, the other children or people may treat him like a secondary member of the family. This creates a constant trauma in the mind (sometimes visible), thus unbalancing the worldview and perceptions of the child that will reflect in his behaviour throughout life.

Here, I would like to share another example. A colleague was trapped in a CBI case and all his promotions were struck down. Many times, he conveyed to me that people had started maintaining distance from him, were talking to him less, thought poorly of him and said things behind his back. Even when I couldn't keep my promise of meeting him, he felt that I was discriminating against him because of the case.

Take the example of a boy who faced continuous failures in life, in relationships and in his career, thereby leading to a distorted perception of the world as a 'mean place'. He continually swears at the world in his conversations or his mind, thus strengthening his belief system, his behaviour and suspicions. Once, he told me that whenever his frustration and suspicions grew, he would develop a mild OCD wherein he would sit in a car, checking and rechecking if the doors were closed or not. This, he said, was an indication to him that he was on the wrong track, and so in reaffirmations, whenever he started repeating that the world is a good place and people around him are good and lovable, his mild OCD symptoms started to disappear.

Another example is that of a lady who was in conflict with her mother-in-law, complaining that she was inflicted by emotional abuse and trauma through derogatory remarks, which she could not forget. Any thought of the mother-in-law (who is still alive) upsets her. In this case, we need to be emotionally intelligent. Conflict can only arise if you consider the opposite party as being of the same calibre or higher than yours. The arguments that the opposite party makes are the product of their character. You can easily see how much love deficit there is in the mother-in-law, and how insecure and emotionally stressed she is. The mother-in-law is also abusing her body, which the daughter-in-law is not noticing. Such people who are insecure and emotionally stressed become more prone to diseases. Absorbing this understanding may help the daughter-in-law to overcome the trauma.

We over-interfere in our children's lives even when they are adults and keep on trying to guide them because we think they are still immature. Parents do this because of excessive care/possessiveness or insecurities about their children so that they don't get hurt. Rather than making their children independent, parents isolate the child and take decisions for them even though they may be married, which leads to conflicts with the children's spouses. But, children will become mature only after taking some wrong decisions in life. My friend Lucky's (name changed) relationship with his mother-in-law illustrates the pitfalls of parents' over-interference in their children's adult lives.

Lucky had a love marriage but started having a troubled life due to the interference of his mother-in-law who was so obsessed and insecure about her daughter that she kept a close vigil on what was happening in her daughter's house on a daily basis.

In one of the events, Lucky and his mother bought a diamond necklace for his wife, and when the wife told her mother that she had been gifted a diamond necklace, Lucky's mother-in-law instantly said, 'See, your in-laws should have consulted you when buying the necklace.' This led to another dispute between the married couple.

This also shows that children who are brought up by insecure (or narcissistic) parents are not independent thinkers.

Lucky's mother-in-law had no mother and was brought up by relatives who treated her harshly, which made her insecure and suspicious. This resulted in her becoming overprotective of her children and always interpreting the action of the children's spouses as conspiracies to humiliate her children. It was no wonder that all her children, three of them altogether, were divorced and remarried, and are still not happy.

So, stay away from the private life of married children. Save your mental health and that of your children too.

A lady (former colleague) was married for four years and had a problem with her husband (everyone will say, 'Who doesn't?'). According to her, he was always dirty, had unkempt hair and his body reeked of a foul odour; even his habits and way of living and behaviour in the family bothered her. She knew he was a good person but the thought of separation from her husband had started ruling her mind. She also felt stiffness in her neck and shoulders. Suspecting a muscular contraction, I told her to consult a doctor as this seemed to be a problem that was connected to her mental state. The doctor prescribed her paroxetine, and in just 3-4 weeks, there was a drastic change in her personality. Her behaviour changed not only towards her spouse but also other people. She was astonished that how such a small medicine could bring about such a difference in her personality. Her parents were equally happy to see her happy with her husband. She and her parents subsequently met the doctor to thank him for healing her, thereby allaying the other issues in her life.

Take a pause and think about similar incident/s that occurred in your life or the life of your near-and-dear ones.

Conspiracy Theory

The human mind is a story processor, not a logic processor.

—Jonathan Haidt

Anthropologists confirm that storytelling is thousands of years old and through this experience, information and knowledge were transferred from one person to another, one group to another, one generation to another.

As per one approximation, when making decisions, humans tend to rely more on the emotional regions of the brain and less on the logical regions. Different kinds of stories trigger different hormones in the body. Heroic stories induce testosterone, romantic triggers oxytocin and stressful or frightening stories induce adrenaline. So, storytelling and its attached meanings work at the level of instinct in human beings.

This same instinct of learning through stories applies when your world reality gets distorted by some sort of acute trust deficit in relationships when you start taking small events happening to you in a negative way and start proving that all the events are being targeted at you. For example, when a student started staying in the college hostel, he began suspecting that his friends and the college staff were working against him. So, he started putting together all the events that happened to him into a story to prove his point that he was being targeted, and that the world was conspiring against him.

What is love?

Love is the best feeling, which we also require for our survival. Love brings about union. However, when someone falls obsessively in love, then it becomes lovesickness. Most of us have faced romantic love in our lives at least once, and for most of us, it has been a good or an average experience. But for some, it has been a bitter experience, and there were also some who lost their lives in its wake.

Obsessive love is being medically studied as an actual illness, when you go up to the level of overthinking, attempting suicide, damaging yourself for the sake of another person, destroying your or their reputation, creating havoc or indulging in emotional self-abuse.

In a study conducted by Italian psychiatrist Donatella

Marazziti,[2] it was found that when people fall into obsessive love, the approximate serotonin levels drop to the levels found in patients with OCD. This level is considerably lower than that of healthy people. The exact reasons why this happens are not known. It may be a way our body works to attract people to reproduce, which is essential for the human race to survive.

> Symptoms of lovesickness may include nausea, concentration issues, under-eating or over-eating, depression, hopelessness, helplessness, inflated or deflated self-esteem, insomnia, possessiveness, abnormal overthinking and rapid mood swings.
> As there is no data available on this, these symptoms are usually misdiagnosed for various mental health issues such as OCD. Therefore, the diagnosis should be taken more seriously.

Love is a complex phenomenon and so is lovesickness, which may be the result of other underlying issues such as depression or anxiety or disharmony in neurotransmitters. **We must focus on physical exercise. We must also correct the gut by changing our food habits (as discussed in Chapter 6) and seek medical advice if needed.**

> The irony is that we celebrate obsessive, one-sided love, as portrayed in Bollywood movies, instead of focussing on and striving for a healthy relationship in which both parties are equally committed. When a loved one passes away, it's normal to mourn. But, if you are not coming out of trauma or are getting worse even after a considerable time period, say, six

[2]Pozza, Andrea, Silvia Casale, Donatella Marazziti, Umberto Albert, Federico Mucci, Erika Berti, Giacomo Grassi, Davide Prestia, and Davide Dèttore, 'Attachment Styles and Propensity for Sexual Response in Adult Obsessive–Compulsive Disorder', *Sexual and Relationship Therapy*, 28 March 2021, https://doi.org/10.1080/14681994.2021.1900805. Accessed on 16 July 2023.

months to one year, then you need counselling or medical help. Such is the level of awareness in our society. Take the Bollywood movie *Kabir Singh* for example. The protagonist Kabir is a doctor and is in so much grief after his girlfriend marries someone else that he indulges in excessive drinking, smoking and drugs, but doesn't consult a psychiatrist or get treated for it.

Tip: Never lose an opportunity to appreciate the best qualities of others. It will give you pleasure and add to your relationships.

Now think of specific people around you and compulsorily find their positive qualities. Ignore the bad qualities. The more you practice, the more of a habit this becomes.

Don't fall for the fallacy of practicality that finding fault in yourself and others is necessary. Being practical is good but it could have a negative impact over a period of time. Your first thoughts should be positive (we will discuss this in detail in subsequent chapters).

The best thing would be to avoid conflict as much as possible. People who keep engaging in conflict are messed up themselves and would pay the price for it by impoverishing the quality of their mental or physical health or getting involved in their issues. They lack love in their lives, so they damage themselves and others. Be emotionally intelligent, have compassion for them and move on.

Trap 5: Feeling out of control

As we age, our body becomes weak, our mobility decreases, our senses become weak, we retire and our children become financially and emotionally independent. Our children don't need us any longer and we are done with our professional lives. There is a sense of being unwanted that slowly starts bothering some of us. This is called loss of autonomy. So, older people do have a greater chance of drifting towards depression or other mental ailments that family members do not know of, and thus, the complications start growing.

Loss of autonomy

Anger or frustration is usually triggered when you become aware that the current situation is out of your control. When the sense of autonomy is lost, it leads to anger or rage. Suppose you have to deal with a situation in which you have no control. If you can't control how your children or seniors and juniors behave with you, there is a temporary spike in frustration. Frustration is also triggered when reality does not match your expectations.

Similarly, when you lose autonomy and feel threatened (this may be real or imaginary), anger/insecurity is triggered. Suppose when you hear some deteriorating remarks about yourself or when someone abuses you, then your ego perceives it as a danger to you and anger is triggered.

> Not eating at the right time is nothing but giving rise to anxiety and anger in your body. The body and brain consider not receiving food as an emergency and as a threat to itself; thus, it turns on the fight-or-flight response, which leads to anger/anxiety/rage. So, it's always better to stick to timings rather than kicking the body to switch on the fight-or-flight response. And when you don't follow a routine, this will damage your psychological system too.

In my previous job, a very senior officer, at one point in time, had struggled through a vigilance case for a long time and started developing mental–emotional issues. Once he was passing by the canteen when he saw two junior officers laughing and having lunch. He went up to them and criticized them, saying that they were talking about him and laughing. Then, he asked these two junior officers to sit separately. This was one of the instances of his paranoia. However, whenever the same senior officer was with his senior, his behaviour was quite different—friendly, docile and filled with overwhelming hospitality.

Let's take another example of how the loss of independence attacks you. If you have a gastrointestinal problem, you would need a toilet whenever your anxiety is triggered. Such a person may develop a fear of going to places where they cannot find a toilet, which means they may develop anxiety issues to the extent that they would avoid going to public places. This is called phobia. Other examples of phobia are:

when an air passenger starts worrying about what will happen if the pilot gets a heart attack or if someone hijacks the plane or if the plane crashes and so on. This can also be seen from a loss of autonomy perspective. When you know your life is in the hands of someone else whom you don't know and the technology of aircraft can fail at any time, then it can set off a panic attack.

Then there is the example of generalized anxiety disorder. A candidate was preparing for a tough exam. In order to crack it, he used his frustration and anxiety to work even harder. The duration of the exam with many levels to it was very long, but despite many failed attempts, he cleared it. But anxiety of a generalized nature had set in him and had begun to take a toll on his health and body. In this case, a fear of performing better was constantly chasing him and he developed a constant feeling of anxiety that he could not control. It became a natural part of him for which he then needed professional help.

Trap 6: Name, fame and status

There was a couple where the man was retired and his wife was still working. They had two daughters; both of them were well-educated. One daughter got married within a year after college, but the marriage didn't work and she got a divorce. The other daughter was around 26 years old at that time and got married against her parent's wishes to a man of her father's age, about 55-60 years old. The father was unhappy with this marriage. He started having digestive problems with a lot of acidity and gastrointestinal pain. When the medication didn't work, he was referred to a psychiatrist to whom he said, 'I don't feel stress/tension in my mind, and my gastric problems have nothing to do with this.' But surprisingly, the psychiatric treatment started working on him. Actually, his mind was negatively affecting his gastric system. It was a crisis of status where he felt that his daughters' current situations were affecting his reputation.

Another example is of a young couple who wanted to get married, but due to the social/caste difference in status, the girl's father vehemently opposed it. As both boy and girl were legally old enough to take a decision, the marriage took place, much against the father's wishes. The couple is now happily settled down and has two children. However, this affected the girl's father significantly as he felt it was a slur on his high social status. This, in turn, led to a gradual deterioration of his health and he remained resentful and angry and refused to meet his daughter, son-in-law and grandchildren. He never got over it and in a span of a few years, he stressed out his body so much that he had multiple organ failure and died. The couple is still living a normal happy life. Thus, not letting go can tear you apart.

A person who is involved in making money and has already accumulated great wealth may still be anxious about the future, forcing him to accumulate even more. If you have nothing else to do and are passionate about making money, it's alright. But when you are running after money, it may be due to insecurity or anxiety driving you. Then surely, it's time to say no to this habit of yours. Usually, in an urge to have better control of the future, insecurity can make you fall or feel sick.

Choose your reference groups wisely

I remember another case wherein a girl kept trying to be a part of a so-called elite group of girls, making them her reference group. She tried to emulate their lifestyle, clothes and behaviour and wanted to party with them. But subconsciously, she was always comparing herself to the other girls in the group. Comparison is the thief of joy.

The issue was that in the girl's mind, she needed to hide her identity and look like the so-called elite girls but was always uncomfortable about it, which made her resentful about her body, attire, personality and her near and dear ones. Gradually, she understood her false thought process and accepted herself the way she was. She felt immensely relieved, like a weight was lifted from her shoulders.

Sometimes you don't realize that you are surrounded by negative friends (maybe parents too). Many times, it is better to stay alone than in bad company. Bad company does not restrain itself to goondas (thugs) but it also means people who have a problem with every situation. You go to them for advice and they only relate negative experiences of their own and others. Remember, negative people are the repositories of negative information and knowledge. Attach yourself to positive people. Read positive quotes. There are always people who will happily guide you but you should know where to get such help or go to a counsellor. But make every effort to stay on the right track.

For example, a person may have strong political viewpoints that may be against the current government because of which they keep overthinking about the future of the nation or keep feeling disgusted with those who support the government. This makes it difficult for them to detach themselves from certain events, even for their own well-being's sake. However, this kind of thinking starts pulling you into a sense of hopelessness, in which case it is better to stop thinking about it. People usually overthink and cannot get rid of their biases, prejudices and experiences they have gained over a period of time.

Trap 7: Unfairness

'Why does this happen only with me? Not a good family background, not a good spouse, my children are not capable. If such and such had happened, I would have been in a better place and situation today. My elder sister got married into a better and wealthier family than mine; I got trapped in a legal case because of my own or someone else's fault...'

Genuine examples of unfairness are: when standing in a queue, you see someone who's late get priority over you because of his connections or regarding reservation for jobs in the government sector, the underprivileged get priority on the basis of caste despite scoring lower marks in the entrance exams. In contrast, the lower caste has an animosity built in over thousands of years that they and their forefathers were forcibly labelled as impure (specifically the Shudras, whom Gandhi called the Harijans in the Indian social/caste system) and were not given equal opportunities. However, having animosity to a certain extent is not diagnosed as a mental illness; the example has been made to make you understand the concept. If you are trapped in this feeling of unfairness that you were victimized, it does start affecting your normal life, and in such cases, you should get out of this cycle.

Suppose a person meets with an accident, and the doctor must amputate one of their legs to save the patient's life. It's always tragic to lose an important body part. After the trauma, the patient can either live complaining about the loss of their leg and keep on feeling sorry for themselves or be thankful that at least their life was saved and focus on better avenues in life. If this person starts complaining repeatedly, it will soon trap them in a mentally sick situation.

There are certain basic things about which we start complaining and comparing ourselves to others whom we think are more fortunate. But remember, comparison is the thief of joy and happiness. Does nature ask you whether you want to be born into a normal or abusive family; black, brown or white; rich or poor? This is all engraved in the system we live in. However, when we start complaining about the system, then mental deterioration starts. Constant complaining is bad for your body and mind, keeping you constantly unhappy.

It simply means that we do not appreciate the existing situation. When we complain and compare, we make ourselves small, feel low and attack our own being. It's giving in to emotional pain. Using comparisons is not a good way of motivating yourself. This way, you increase the threshold of being happy, and keep on postponing the state of happiness. Complaining simply happens when you are not ready to take responsibility for your actions and life situations because of lack of self-confidence.

I had the blues because I had no shoes until upon the street, I met a man who had no feet.

–Denis Waitley

(1) You think you're not pretty? Someone is wishing to be as pretty as you.

(2) You want more money? People are living in poverty.

(3) You want a boyfriend/girlfriend? Someone doesn't even have parents.

(4) You're hungry? A child is starving.

(5) You want to go to the mall? Someone is looking for anything to wear just to stay warm.

(6) You're chilly? Others on the street are freezing.

(7) You want to die? Most people are striving to live.

(8) You are not brilliant? Some will be very happy if they have even a little knowledge of something.

(9) You need a car? Some can't even walk on their own feet.

Don't waste your time on things that you think you don't have, because there is always someone out there who needs what you have!

> *Appreciate what life has given you.*
> *Leading a normal life is a blessing.*
>
> –Anonymous
>
> Some people have a persistent negative thought process and feel relaxed after venting their constantly generated frustration, anger, resentment, anxiety and irritation.
>
> Others having constantly negative thought processes start hurting themselves because they are not venting.
>
> When the problem lies within you, then you have to focus on *changing* the basic negative thought process that is behind a major source of venom rather than *controlling* the negative emotional reactions at face value.

In this battle of knowns and unknowns, where we are still not fully aware of *how* and *why* our brain behaves the way it does, what we can be certain about is not allowing our minds to ensnare us. There is some truth to the famous dialogue *Kehte hain agar kisi cheez ko dil se chaaho, toh puri qayanat usse tumse milane ki koshish mein lag jaati hai...* (If you really desire something from your heart, the whole universe will conspire to help you achieve it). Do you want to know how? Then read on…

3

The Successful State of Mind

Nothing great is ever achieved without enthusiasm.

—Ralph Waldo Emerson

Being successful is always desirable. When you put all your energy into working hard, then you need constant inspiration and a vision at the back of your mind. It is that inspiration and vision that is the subject of this chapter, and which can shape the mindset of a person, either positively or negatively, in the long run—leading to a 'successful' state of our minds.

We have often come across success stories of people who say that they achieved success because they could channel the negative events of their lives into a positive force that pushed them towards success, and no doubt they overcame their obstacles and turned stumbling blocks into stepping stones.

So, how do we conjure up the fundamental force that takes you closer to success?

There are two ways of mobilizing ourselves to work hard. One way of achieving this is to make ourselves uncomfortable in the current position by means of negative feelings like frustration, anger, etc., so that we can motivate ourselves to leave the current situation and jump to new positions of success. This is called a **push strategy** as we are trying to push ourselves by way of generating bad feelings and then channelizing them for achieving success.

Another way is when you use the **pull strategy**, which means you are at point A in life and you want to go to point B (e.g. higher social position), then you start loving point B so much that you remain motivated to achieve success in reaching B. This second viewpoint can help in avoiding unnecessary and unintended bodily and mental harm that can be inflicted by your mind using a negative narrative to mobilize you.

Both strategies may bring you success but the former, by its very fundamental nature, will reinforce the negative patterns of bad feelings in you. In the end, our brain is just a complex group of self-learning neurons. Once you get successful using the former model, the same patterns of negative emotional reactions will keep reappearing or permanently become a part of your personality (like general anxiety or psychosomatic disorders). The former model of success comes at a cost that will bring down your quality of life by way of silently and slowly killing your body and mental well-being.

> When I was on medication (selective serotonin reuptake inhibitors [SSRIs] type of medication), with the increase in the availability of serotonin (adequate serotonin), my mind was automatically working with interest (pull strategy), and when I was low on serotonin, it wasn't interested in work, so I had to use the push strategy.
>
> That was a revelation. When your brain is in a healthy condition, you don't usually need motivation from outside, it comes from within.

COMMON CAUSES OF UNHAPPINESS

Relationships

- When there is a breakup or a divorce
- Death of a near one
- Death of children, issues in the lives of children
- Feeling of being cheated
- Disillusionment

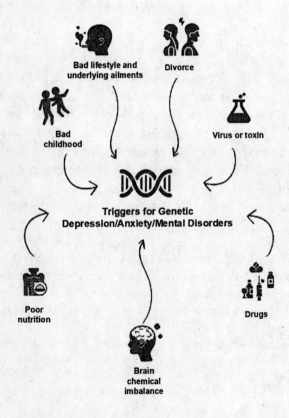

Biological Factors

- Attention deficit hyperactivity disorder (ADHD) in parents passed on to the child
- Underlying unknown inflammation(s), which may be caused by an as-yet-undiagnosed food allergy

Socialization and Upbringing

- Learning from corrupt people in the community
- Influenced by family/caste discrimination or sects/cults

Lifestyle

- No physical activity
- No regular work that excites you or triggers your curiosity
- Lack of sleep, unhealthy diet

SYMPTOMS OF DEPRESSION

- Living in escapist thoughts (including excessive usage of phones)
- Irritation
- Receding from social life
- Excessive dependence on harmful addictions like alcohol
- Excessive smoking or using drugs
- Lack of concentration
- Constantly remaining angry, frustrated, anxious
- Procrastinating excessively at work
- When you think you are being practical but people around you say that you are being too negative
- Eating too much or too little
- Frequent headaches, back and neck pain, mood swings, sleeping problems, nightmares, frequent urination, gastric problems due to anxiety/stress
- Unnecessary emotional overreaction or feeling emotionally numb
- Nervous habits (grinding teeth, biting nails, etc.)
- Constant insecurity about self and loved ones
- Your facial expression shows stress or unhappiness
- General fatigue, even if you are eating what you normally eat
- Falling in obsessive love with someone
- Developing OCD
- Not giving anyone the benefit of the doubt, jumping to conclusions
- Blaming ourselves for everything
- Excessive suspicion
- Abnormally good and bad hygiene
- Becoming excessively controlling at work or home, i.e. being a narcissist

- Constantly feeling apologetic
- Sense of hopelessness
- Constant feelings of victimization
- Being unable to easily forget/forgive and holding grudges for a long time

All the above symptoms indicate unhealthy traits that should be tackled as soon as possible to achieve a 'successful' state of mind. The more positive thoughts you have, the more mentally healthy you are; the more negative thoughts you have, the more you should question your well-being.

The above list of causes and symptoms is not exhaustive. Read it again and tick off those that you feel are relevant. Or you can add your causes and symptoms as well. You can also use the above points to check if people around you are showing similar symptoms but note that you should not label/judge them.

Now, in continuation of the above, we will try to identify the symptoms for you to start self-diagnosing them. This mental health literacy is for all, for a better understanding of ourselves and others.

Are you trapped in the loop of postponing happiness?

It's good to make plans and execute them, but many times we keep on sabotaging them ourselves by having thoughts like, 'I will do this after the children get married, after their education, after a salary hike, after retirement, and so on.' In this way, we are unknowingly *furthering our threshold* for happiness—if I get this car, that promotion etc.—and not giving reasons to our brain to get stimulated to be happy.

Some keep on channelizing their past pains and failures into challenging themselves to push further towards success, which has its own disadvantages.

> Keep the above fact in mind to strike a balance in favour of happiness rather than sabotaging yourself.
>
> Note that there is no simple way to stop procrastinating, it will vanish when you understand yourself and reset your gut (as we will be discussing in Chapter 6).

WHAT PULLS THE TRIGGER?

Our mind works on precedence, on subconscious and conscious learned patterns in the distant and near past, especially in childhood, which we may not even be aware of. We may have forgotten the details. We make generalizations and extrapolations, so be suspicious of your first impulse— why is it happening to you? Say, you see a person whose face resembles a person who wronged you at some point in time. This can be the trigger where you start recollecting all bad memories and become angry. Another example would be an officer getting triggered by the posture of an employee sitting in front of him and exaggerating the behaviour as disobedience, which may not be the intent of the employee. Nevertheless, such misunderstandings may trigger the officer into a fit of rage.

Write Down Your Possible Triggers

Suppose one day you wake up and something triggers you, putting you in a bad mood as you start remembering things that happened to you in the past. You will start your day feeling resentful, angry and negative. These unwanted weeds (feelings) in your garden (mind) take up unnecessary space and if these persist for too long, these negative feelings can get embedded in you and become your personality traits.

As a result, in your radar system, you perceive an incoming bird as a fighter jet about to bomb you, and you are instantly in fight-or-flight mode, becoming either overactive or underactive. Your fear and frustrations get magnified; and when your driver does not reach on time, for example, an overwhelming feeling of anger may be triggered.

Frequent anger leads to high levels of cortisol, which usually remains in the body. These chemicals also release fatty acids that keep accumulating in the blood vessels and may lead to cardio and other health issues over a long period of time.

Now, write down your possible triggers, and then we will learn how to handle them.

_____

_____

_____

_____

_____

_____

Handling Triggers

Once a saint wanted to meditate but he was finding it very difficult as he was being disturbed quite frequently. This made him angry with himself and others around him. So he took a boat and went into the middle of the lake, feeling sure that nobody would disturb him there, and closed his eyes to meditate. After a while, he felt a jerk in his boat and again became angry. Now who had disturbed him? When he opened his eyes, he saw another boat, which was empty, but the water flow had caused it to come into contact with his boat. He then realized what the issue was. The problem was inside rather than outside his mind, making him overreact and disturbing his peace of mind.

Similarly, many situations in life can be handled by not reacting and just ignoring them. Not every situation requires a reaction—overreaction, not at all.

Triggers Due to Punch Lines

1. I know what they are thinking about me.
2. People don't like me.
3. They are talking about my recent activity.
4. They are impractical as they talk about always being 'positive', I am 'practical'.
5. Everyone gossips.
6. The world is a f*****-up place.

Arguments

When another person keeps arguing, it does not mean that they are emotionally intelligent. The rational response is to just say, 'Yes, you are right,' and leave the topic. Walk away. Discussion rather than argument is the desired mode of interaction.

Why do we absorb negativity faster?

Media and social media affect the amygdala, the part of the brain that emotes feelings of sex, violence, hunger and desire. That is why there is so much negative propaganda. The brain catches negative feelings, especially threats, (as negative experiences are stored in the hippocampus) so that it can react and defend itself. This basic instinct of the body to save itself is exploited by the media to keep us glued to their news.

ARE YOU TAKING THINGS PERSONALLY?

Taking things personally can be a serious cause for resentment and anxiety. For some readers, this may not be a serious issue, but for some, it does become a serious matter, especially if they keep thinking or judging everything.

Another way is to consider that many people are like garbage trucks. They run around full of garbage, frustration, anger and disappointment. As their garbage piles up, they look for a place to dump it. And if you allow them, they'll dump it on you. So, when someone wants to do this, don't take it personally.

Some people who feel insecure think that it is only by giving a befitting reply that the other can be brought down. Such behaviour can be due to childhood socialization in which they were bullied by others, or they have consciously and subconsciously learned that being aggressive and assertive is the only way to get things done. But most of the time, letting go is the best option to end a dispute.

To check if you take things too personally, just write down the events or people that have hurt your ego. The longer the list, the more likely you are to take things personally.

PLEASURE AND HAPPINESS

Our bodies are designed by nature in such a way that we are dependent on our environment. From the moment we are born, we need the care, comfort and security of a mother. Babies feel satisfied when fed or when they are given toys or taken out for walks. They cry if they are not comfortable or are in pain. As they grow, wearing clothes they prefer, looking better, getting high grades and having precious possessions become more important. Then, the focus changes to better education, money, property and spouses—these things run throughout their life. Through this rigorous training of looking for happiness outside, we forget to introspect. Our attention is trained to run after worldly things. If we get those things, we are happy for some time, and then we need more targets to be happy. But just saying that the outside world doesn't count in making us happy is not what I am saying. There has to be a balance.

Like a one-dimensional man, our generation is running after happiness, and there is a growing industry to put you on the path of pleasure rather than happiness. As we have advanced from primitive societies to complex heterogeneous and differentiated societies to make ourselves more comfortable and satisfied, somewhere we are missing out on the basics. That is happiness. Ironically, happiness is today being treated as a goal. It is not a goal but a basic condition to live. It is our primary right to be happy, and to move ahead in life rather than constantly chasing it. That is when life brings us rewards. It is the primary condition that must exist in each of us without effort. Nature has given us an instinct to be happy, but somehow, we have lost ourselves in secondary things.

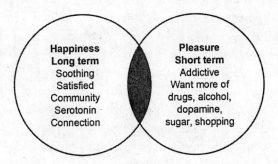

'If you've been told your entire life that pleasure is happiness, then you know, you're screwed,' says Robert Lustig, an American endocrinologist.[3]

For example, months after buying the car you have always wanted, it loses its attraction, getting appreciation from fewer and fewer people. It starts to look a little dirty as you don't care about cleaning and washing it. The car that you once called 'happiness' loses its attraction in just a few months. When you are anticipating a reward, dopamine is at work. But the neurotransmitter dopamine is different from serotonin—the chemical known for happiness. You get dopamine when you get money, but from where does happiness—serotonin—

---

[3] Happiness vs. Pleasure and Why It Matters | by Dr Robert Lustig, YouTube, https://www.youtube.com/watch?v=Ypht2SEIin4. Accessed on 16 May 2023.

come? You can get happiness from wherever you are, but the pleasure will push you to achieve more. We tend to overestimate the pleasure brought by new experiences and underestimate the power of contentment in existing resources. Pleasure is addictive and lasts for a short span of time, but happiness remains for a long time. So, we should prioritize actions and goals in our lives.

Happiness (serotonin) is spread over at least 14 receptors across the brain, whereas dopamine-induced pleasure touches smaller parts of the brain—around five receptors. Pleasure craves for more and happiness gives the feeling of satisfaction. As you keep on scrolling through social media or post your selfies online for likes, that's what the dopamine-related pleasure is doing—keeping you glued to your mobiles. The same works with craving sugar or junk food. Even in drug addiction, in the name of searching for bliss, dopamine is what plays a major role. But do all these things make you content? No.

A person approached Blaise Pascal, a French mathematician, physicist and religious philosopher, and asked him if he had Pascal's brains, would he have been a better person? Pascal replied, 'Just be a better person, and you will have my brains.' So it's about mindset—how free, enthusiastic, curious and creative you are. And that will happen when you will break your mental barriers.

If you have been in an unhappy state for long, you may consider that as being normal and may not be able to judge your current state of unhappiness; many symptoms may start appearing, which you would not even realize, as you were never told about them, and thus, you would start attracting negative mental symptoms. The path to happiness is when you are able to focus more and work systematically; there is a fine balance between your emotional and logical thinking when you feel energetic and are ready to effectively and smoothly perform your tasks.

Don't search for more text here to make you happy. The whole book is only about this.

Drug Addiction and the Mind

> *A shot to kill the pain. A pill to drain the shame.*
> *A purge to end the gain. A cut to break the vein.*
> *A smoke to ease the crave. A drink to win the game.*
> *An addiction is an addiction because it all hurts the same.*

—Anonymous

Just 250 micrograms of lysergic acid diethylamide (LSD) leads to a psychedelic effect, which means that psychedelics affect all the senses—altering a person's thinking, sense of time and emotions, interfering with the serotonin receptors.

STOP TAKING DRUGS

Heavy drugs, such as morphine, heroin and codeine, are the worst drugs on earth because when the opioid receptors—which are used by the endorphins—are released in your brain, you start moving into a world of dark depression, which makes you take the next dose. These drugs make the opiate receptors resistant so that the next time you use them, you'll require a higher dosage for receptors to work.

Social support: During drug de-addiction, social support is extremely important. The brain is hardwired for having social support as it can reduce relapses. Engaging in conversations and social interactions are necessary. The body is made in such a way that when we interact face-to-face, our bodies feel better because we always have been in groups throughout evolution, and this has been tailored into our genes.

Over a period of time, drug abuse decreases oxytocin levels in various areas of the brain, the hypothalamus, hippocampus and nucleus accumbens. That's why to stay away from addiction you will need company and when you have good company, the craving for drugs can decrease. So, social support is an essential requirement.

Remember, alcohol or drugs are your friendly enemies, so if you are working on the idea of drinking or taking drugs to end your sadness, totally banish the thought, because the results will soon become the opposite and you will lose your independence.

THE BATTLE WITHIN

Hero vs. Villain

We all are heroes in our stories. Being good in our eyes is one of our primary instincts. This instinct, if not properly dealt with, can seriously impact our mental health and be one of the main reasons for turning us into an overthinker. When something has gone wrong in your life, like someone has degraded you or deceived you, or you could not achieve what you thought you were capable of, or you are afraid that someone who knows your life's secrets can harm your reputation, you keep on overthinking because your mind cannot digest such facts and settle down. So, you keep struggling and fighting these facts in your mind, consuming much of your mental resources. It, therefore, becomes imperative to accept such facts of life; otherwise, they may gradually put you on a path to mental instability without your knowledge. Let's now discuss how to get out of this situation.

We need to change our perception regarding any conflict that is messing up our minds. It's important to know that a number of positive or just neutral thoughts keep passing through the mind with your knowledge but most of the time it's without your knowledge. But, when any thought that is negative or is against your ego or which you (as a hero of your story) don't want to make part of your life story, then the struggle starts, overthinking happens and you end up wasting your energy and time struggling with it and find it extremely difficult to focus on other important issues.

Given this challenge, the simplest and most effective way is to change the negative feelings attached to the fact/issue that is disturbing you to positive ones. So, use positive affirmations/visualizations, logic and other methods (discussed in the following text) to convert such negativities into positive or neutral facts. Say, if someone has wronged us in the past, instead of thinking about ways to get revenge, we can think positively in terms of how we may have achieved something because of that incident or may have gained certain experiences that are relevant now.

Some of us may feel guilty, shameful or fearful because of some of our past acts. These can be resolved in the same way as discussed above, that is, convert those facts into positive versions. We have to let go. We should give space to ourselves and try to understand that perhaps we were just not strong enough then to act wisely. Give yourself the benefit of ignorance and weak understanding, and the onus can be shifted to situations that have passed rather than you in the present moment.

Let's move on to more important ways of re-engineering our mind and tuning it to the best frequency. If we are trapped in a mental prison, the doors often open only from the inside. Take the example of Varun who had a complicated relationship with his girlfriend. They broke up because both accused each other of misconduct and misunderstanding. Now, after a decade, Varun started harping on the idea that had she (his ex-girlfriend) not misbehaved, they would have been happily married. This thought became so strong in him that it was haunting him and making him angry. It was a bag of mixed emotions but it was intense. Upon getting some advice, however, his perception of his ex-girlfriend started changing. Varun could not only see her positively but also affirm that whatever happened between them was due to uncontrolled situations and immaturity. If anyone else could have been in that situation, a similar outcome or worse could have happened. Soon, neither were the thoughts of his ex-girlfriend nagging him anymore nor was he feeling guilty as he had come out of the overthinking loop.

We must first shed the ostrich syndrome, that is, recognize the problem, because only then can we move ahead. If you recognize it but don't know how to get out, or don't have the discipline and will to make the change, you keep moving in survival mode and forget to live happily.

◆

Benefit of the Doubt

The major reason for misjudging is that the benefit of the doubt is not considered while thinking. How can we understand this in terms of cognitive behavioural therapy? Let's explore this in the following section.

Cognitive Behavioural Therapy

> *The significant problems we face cannot be solved at the same level of thinking we were at when we created them.*
>
> —Arie de Geus

Battling smoke without battling the fire is like battling mental illness without changing the thought process and belief system at the core.

The biggest advantage for our brain is its neuroplasticity. Whether we are middle-aged or old, we still retain this capability to reform our minds; it's a constant process. We can still change our beliefs and emotional thoughts. No one can destroy iron except its own rust. Likewise, no one can destroy a person except their own mind.

Many depressed patients don't know what cognitive behavioural therapy is, and so, they have not even tried it. It is not popular as there is no big marketing budget to inform patients about it. It needs to be highlighted and its impact needs to be observed in the long term. It is much better than depending on medicines. It is cheap in the long run and there are no side-effects. Even I came to know about it after a long time.

We need to understand that thought has two parts:

- **Cognition**, which refers to mental processing, including thinking, knowing, remembering, judging and problem-solving.
- **Physiological component**, in which the cognition by the brain leads to effects on body parts like increased heartbeat, sweating, upset stomach, rapid breathing, etc.

The medicine that is taken to resolve such issues works only on the physiological component and not on the cognitive component, but the latter can sometimes be the root cause. When we stop the medicine, the symptoms will reappear. That means we need to work on the cognition aspect that changes bad perceptions, imaginations and thought processes. While taking medicines helps, it may be cognition where the actual cause may reside.

The difference between belief and cognition is that the former is a feeling that somebody/something is true, morally good or right or that somebody/something really exists, while the latter is the process by which knowledge and understanding are developed in the mind. At the core is belief, because if there are negative beliefs, it will lead to negative interpretations and emotions and trigger a series of thoughts that will again strengthen our negative belief system.

Say, you believe that people around you are cleverer and will take advantage of you. You will start feeling insecure, suspicious and anxious, which will trigger a series of thoughts wherein you will start relating previous events and will extrapolate on forthcoming events. This, in turn, will strengthen your negative belief system that people around you are cleverer and will take advantage of you.

And so, the vicious circle goes on, and whenever you are free or under pressure or some situation arises, this vicious loop will keep working. If it is a decade-old loop you are trapped in, you may have been through it a million times, knowingly or unknowingly.

Breaking this negative belief system is at the core of cognitive behavioural therapy, and may help in preventing a relapse.

◆

Let's see how people in the same situation act differently according to their belief systems.

Ramesh ignored you. Now, you may feel angry or worthless; so, you will either self-deprecate or feel jealous, have hurt sentiments, feel guilty, anxious, revengeful, irritable, frustrated, ashamed or may think, 'I don't care.'

Depending on our level of maturity or power to ignore, which is interconnected with our mental and gut health (about which we will read in Chapter 6), this situation can be tackled without negative emotional overreaction. Changing our reaction as per the situation means changing our belief system, which is at the core of behavioural reaction. However, changing a person's belief system may be extremely difficult because:

a) they believe they are right.
b) they believe they are practical.
c) they believe they have that experience.
d) they have drawn conclusions by noticing other people.
e) they have gathered information from books, media and social media.
f) they have been informed by a person in whom they have faith.

◆

(a) Spat between spouses

How has this developed? One or both may think that the other ignores them (there may have been similar instances in the past).

Trigger	Belief	Consequences 1. Emotional consequence 2. Psychological consequence 3. Physical consequence	Deleting dysfunctional thoughts and adding new positive thoughts	Effect
Wife says to husband: You don't know how to feed the baby	**Husband's belief:** The wife wants to settle scores by demeaning him	1. Anger or revenge 2. Overreaction and overthinking 3. Blood pressure rises or breathing becomes irregular	**Dysfunctional thought:** She is doing it intentionally **New positive thought:** Maybe the husband is not able to feed the child properly or is not able to feed the child the way the wife considers right (affirming such thoughts continuously will start showing positive results)	No anger and no overthinking

(b) Overthinking about cardiac arrest

How has this developed? Someone in the family may have experienced a heart attack, which is usually followed by information-gathering from other people and the internet, thereby reaching self-made conclusions such as 'My heart rate increases when I climb stairs, play, etc.' by comparing with other people around us, resulting in excessive thoughts about the same and it becoming a belief system.

Trigger	Belief	Consequences 1. Emotional consequence 2. Psychological consequence 3. Physical consequence	Deleting dysfunctional thoughts and adding new positive thoughts	Effect
Exercising and feeling chest pain	Many people get a heart attack while exercising	1. Anxiety attack or seizure 2. Overthinking and reinforcing the belief that it can be a heart attack 3. Everything goes dark, breathlessness and physical pain around the chest	**Logic:** Is this chest pain or a heart attack? **Divergent view:** It can just be fake pain or anxiety (affirming such thoughts continuously will start showing positive results)	Won't overreact

(c) People gossip about me

How has this developed? You may remember innumerable instances in your life when you may have walked into your group of friends or colleagues having a hearty laugh, whereupon you may have thought that they were laughing about you. In reality, it could have been any number of other things.

Trigger	Belief	Consequences 1. Emotional consequence 2. Psychological consequence 3. Physical consequence	Deleting dysfunctional thoughts and adding new positive thoughts	Effect
Two or more people are laughing	Poor self-image and insecurity; therefore, such people assume that others are talking about and making fun of them	1. Resentment, anger or irritation 2. Overthinking 3. May fight with people they suspect or complain about them to higher authorities	**Divergent view:** They have other issues to discuss and laugh about (affirming such thoughts continuously will start showing positive results)	No overreaction

(d) Different phobias and fears

How has this developed? A fear or phobia can be:

- Social, such as stage fear, being in crowds.
- Psychological, such as fear of contracting a disease like coronavirus, flu, etc.
- Based on other factors, such as travelling by air, aircraft, exam-related phobia, etc.

Dog phobia

Trigger	Belief	Consequences 1. Emotional consequence 2. Psychological consequence 3. Physical consequence	Deleting dysfunctional thoughts and adding new positive thoughts	Effect
Sighting of dog	Dogs are animals and hence unpredictable; they will surely run after and bite me	1. Fear 2. Overthinking or feeling insecure 3. Yelling at the dog or walking or running away, which makes the dog follow the person	**Dysfunctional thought:** Dogs will chase and bite me **New positive thought:** Dogs are good creatures (affirming such thoughts continuously will start showing positive results)	It will change your body language and hence, the dog's reaction will change for you.

Aircraft phobia

Trigger	Belief	Consequences 1. Emotional consequence 2. Psychological consequence 3. Physical consequence	Deleting dysfunctional thoughts and adding new positive thoughts	Effect

| Travelling by air | Travelling by air is risky, lots of plane crashes are happening | 1. Phobia 2. Overthinking, fear or insecurity 3. Faster heartbeat, avoiding aircraft travelling or sweating | **Dysfunctional thought:** Travelling by air is risky **New positive thought:** Travelling by air is the safest; read about its safety from various sources like the internet, others are also travelling and they are all happy, calm and safe (affirming such thoughts continuously will start showing positive results) | Body and mind won't negatively overreact |

(e) Insecurity

How has this developed? Whether it be our upbringing or the way our society has conditioned us, we may have numerous insecurities that rear their ugly heads from time to time.

Trigger	Belief	Consequences 1. Emotional consequence 2. Psychological consequence 3. Physical consequence	Deleting dysfunctional thoughts and adding new positive thoughts	Effect

| My daughter-in-law has said that she will move houses | People around me are clever and will take advantage of me | 1. Anger, feeling of losing their son who will settle with daughter-in-law 2. Thinking suspiciously that mother-in-law-may hatch her own conspiracy to tackle the situation 3. Any psychosomatic disorder | 1. My daughter-in-law will take care of us 2. The daughter-in-law may have a different notion in mind 3. The new house may benefit all (affirming such thoughts continuously will start showing positive results) | No overreaction, stress or resentment. |

Exercise: Write about one of your issues here

Trigger	Belief	Consequences 1. Emotional consequence 2. Psychological consequence 3. Physical consequence	Deleting dysfunctional thoughts and adding new positive thoughts	Effect

The crux of the above text is to broaden your intellect or think from other people's perspective, which may help you in solving your negative emotional overreactions and improve your thought process. That is, be more emotionally intelligent.

Think about other people's situations before jumping to a conclusion. You may not be aware of their situation or perspective; sometimes, allow yourself to ignore certain reactions if needed.

And this brings us to the next step in our journey, where we will learn to embrace positivity and refrain from negativity.

4

The Habit of Visualizing Happiness

Being happy doesn't mean that everything is perfect. It means you've decided to look beyond the imperfection.

—Gerard Way

Our relationships, behaviour with ourselves and others, overthinking and critical thinking about the past, present and future depend upon the main focus of our mind—our general perspective. In this chapter, we will be discussing this general perspective and focus on visualizing happiness. **The focus is to bring about a change in our instant reactions to people, situations/issues, from negative to positive.**

MY EXPERIENCE

The interview conducted by the Union Public Service Commission is said to be one of the toughest interviews to prepare for. I was searching for some personality development tips while preparing for the same. Improving your personality for just an interview is not easy when you have been repeating the traits of your current personality all your life. Therefore, I needed help to transform my personality. My college friend, Ankur Jarora, was known for acing every interview he ever sat for; he also had a very positive aura that we could feel while talking to him. So, we fixed up a meeting. That sunny day, we took a drive to the nearby hills. He straightaway asked me to speak on the positive aspects of some specific welfare schemes for two minutes, to which I replied with two to three positive statements, but soon got exhausted, in just 20 or 30 seconds, and instead, I started speaking about the problems and loopholes in the scheme, such as corruption, leakages, etc.

Here, Ankur interrupted me. He said, 'You were not asked to speak about the negative aspects of the scheme. And so soon you have ended up focussing on its limitations. Note the compulsion of your mind to think negatively about something after just two or three lines.'

Although I had to mention the positive aspects of something, my personality trait has always been to think negatively. However, this trait had to be reversed; our minds should always keep looking for positive things automatically.

WHAT IS THIS TECHNIQUE ALL ABOUT?

This technique can be very useful in determining your thought process or someone else's. Thereafter, you can identify and initiate changes in yourself for good. Just think of a certain event, a specific person or an object around you and observe what comes to your mind instantly. Is it positive or negative? Whatever thought (positive/negative) first comes to your mind without effort shows your (positive/negative) thought process.

Now, try to think positively for at least 1-2 minutes. See if the first thought you have is negative. Or, after 2-3 thoughts regarding the strengths, did you start thinking about the flaws? If yes, then that's an alarm bell, which indicates that you need to change your thought process for your mental health and peace of mind.

It is important to note that a constant thinking process goes on in our minds; thoughts keep moving in and out of our minds with/without our knowledge. If we have a negative thought process regarding certain issues/objects/events, negative reactions will be triggered in our minds. We can't stop this but we do have the power to change the nature of our thoughts to a positive stream. We cannot control our minds but rather channel them to keep focussing on positive ideas.

WHY DOES THE BRAIN USE PROTOTYPES?

The brain wants to work at a lower voltage, i.e. it tries to save energy every time it sees the same thing. So, it forms habits, prejudices and biases. It forms ideal-type patterns or generalized views. It avoids rediscovering the same things. Therefore, it tries to impose already known habits, biases and prejudices on people, issues and situations. If you feel negative about some issues/events in your life, rather than rediscovering them from a positive angle, your brain will try to impose a negative pattern on them. You will be at ease by thinking negatively about a particular thing. For example, after a few people from a particular region misbehave with a person 3-4 times, this person may start having prejudgements about all people from that particular region. The brain is a miser by nature. This sort of shutting down of the mind to avoid rediscovery makes the person's approach narrower. Further, a habit of jumping to conclusions and a tendency to steer clear of exploring new things develop.

As children, we were more flexible, but as we age, we become more rigid and make prototypes. We gather experiences and inferences and start calling these things practical. As we grow old, we see the limitations, hard practicalities of life, fewer resources, bad relationships and so many other things that makes everything feel more terrible than it actually is. We put on the veil of hardness and our thoughts somehow become negative in the guise of practicality. If something has gone wrong with someone in certain aspects of life, it does not mean it will happen to everyone. In the guise of being practical, we close down the windows of the mind and the air of reason doesn't circulate which, with age, may lead to mental ailments. **So be open, practical, learn how your mind works and think positively for your sake.**

BARRIERS THAT STOP YOU

'How can I forgive those who did horrible things to me? It is not practical!'

The barrier that will stop you from thinking positively about every issue/person/event in life will be your gained experience, which has become a part of your ego and personality. Who wants to think about themselves as being wrong? The negative conclusions you have drawn are very dear to you and are so much a part of yourself that you can't throw them away. It's like downsizing yourself.

We may say that thinking positively every time is not practical. How can we think well of a person who has harmed us? How can we forgive?

Here, we must remember that we are being told to forgive but not forget. We must also know that by forgiving, we are not relieving the person who did horrible things to us, but we are forgiving ourselves. For example, when Arun forgave a friend against whom he had a grudge in the past, Arun was actually forgiving himself. It was the mental image of Arun's friend that was creating trouble for him because whenever he thought of the friend, the neural pattern representing the friend in Arun's mind was fired, causing agony, frustration, anger and resentment in him. So, when Arun forgave the friend (by turning his friend's negative image to a neutral/positive one in his mind), he came out of a vicious overthinking loop. Being constantly angry with someone in your mind is similar to holding a burning coal in your hands and expecting the enemy to get harmed.

Thus, forgiving means not punishing yourself for someone else's misdeeds.

HOW TO GO ABOUT THIS?

> *Bullea rabb da ki pavana etho putna uthe laavna.*
> *(How to get God is as simple as channelizing your*
> *attention from one worldly affair to another.)*

—Shah Inayat Qadri

Just think of topics, events and issues revolving around your life and make a conscious effort to think about them positively. For example, think of a plant in your garden—it gives oxygen, biomass, fruits, shelter to insects, etc. Think about going to a distant land like South Africa. Think about the clock hanging on your wall…then think about the negative events of your life, and now force yourself to think positively about what they have taught you.

Remember, you have to make it a habit of thinking positively without any effort. Positive thoughts should flow automatically.

Make a list of all things you hate	Now think about them positively
1.	
2.	
3.	
4.	
5.	
6.	
7.	
8.	
9.	
10.	

Repeat this in your free time and you will unload a lot of unnecessary baggage from your mind. Also remember, the greater the resistance of your mind to be positive about some issue/event, the greater the love and healing is required for you to change.

ANOTHER PERSONAL EXPERIENCE

While preparing for a mock interview, someone on the panel asked me a question on a certain topic that had been covered by the editorial section of a newspaper two or three days earlier. I also had the habit of reading the reactions of readers the next day, which used to be usually negative and against the government policy. But, when the question was asked by the mock interview panel, I started speaking positively and instantly I started reproducing the negative comments as the limitations. This meant that my mind was attracting and remembering negative things without any effort.

After I realized this, I stopped reading the reaction box of editorials and that prevented negative arguments from entering my mind. This process is subtle. So, even if you say that you will just read negative arguments without absorbing them, it's a myth. Be firm and say no to negative content wherever you read or see it; you are not smarter than your mind. (Remember Gandhiji's Three Monkeys—see no evil, speak no evil, hear no evil. Gandhiji's message runs deeper than we imagine.)

The other major shift occurred when I was reading *Imagining India* by Nandan Nilekani. It's about changing the concept and idea of India, how India is transforming and how our general understanding about India is changing with time. The first chapter was positive and as I read half the book and saw the author speaking positively about every aspect of the country, even when there were many problems, I thought, 'Is this the practical way to approach a conceptualization of India? Isn't it too impractical?' Then, after introspecting, I found that in the guise of becoming practical, negative ideas strike me very easily. While thinking about the positive aspects, I have to make an effort with my mind. Why not reverse the trend? Then, I forced myself to think positively about everything around me and after a while, I was at ease about doing so on some days. I really thank this book for changing my thought process.

> Even while reading other books, if you come across any negativities, just skip it, and do the same with other news/social media. Remember Gandhiji's saying: 'I will not *let anyone* walk through *my mind* with *their* dirty feet', i.e. we should never allow anyone to bother us with their negativity, whether through oral or written medium.

FIRST THOUGHT TECHNIQUE

Think of anything—past, present or future—and compulsorily think positively about it.

Exercise

Think positively about the following so that your natural flow becomes positive, i.e. positive thoughts must strike you straight away.

Your career
Your siblings
Your past failures

Your college
Strict teachers
Car model
Plants
Leaves
Thorns
Cow dung
Bedsheet
Democracy
Dictatorship
Horror movie
Hospital patient
Fan
Table
Your boss whom you feel has wronged you in the office

Point to ponder!

Let's take another example of Arun, who started writing the names of all those whom he thought had harmed him so that he could keep a record and take revenge later on. He wrote around 20-25 names. After a while, he realized that the problem actually lay within himself. It's okay to have issues with 3-4 people, but Arun's list had become too long. He too became aware of this, which became a trigger for his self-realization and self-improvement.

(The moot point is that if your list of 'enemies' is too long, you should introspect and more often than not, you will observe that the problem may be lying with you.)

AFFIRMATIONS

…what you resist not only persists, but will grow in size.

—Carl Gustav Jung

Affirmations are another powerful way in which we can re-engineer the emotions attached to words and sentences and visualize happiness. Each word has a feeling or emotion attached to it; thus, we will be using more positive words and staying away from negative emotions.

If you eat infected food, your stomach will react abnormally. The same is the situation with the mind. It needs positive food, i.e. positive thoughts. Similarly, in these affirmations, we need to use repetitions to convince our subconscious minds. We essentially need healthy nutrition by way of positive thoughts.

However, due to our ignorance or bad experiences or toxic upbringing, we unintentionally keep using negative affirmations that make/keep our minds sick. After consuming infected food, we usually suffer from a bloated stomach, vomiting or constipation. Similarly, when we consume bad thoughts for a long period of time, that sickness may manifest itself in the form of excessive frustration, anxiety, irritation and depression.

Our bodies hear everything that our tongues and minds say to themselves and others, so stay positive and be kind. If you say that you can have double standards—one becoming positive to yourself and the other becoming negative to others—or vice-versa, then frankly, this is not possible. Either you are good or you are bad. If you are good to yourself, you have to be good to others and if you are bad to yourself, you have to be the same to others too. Let's see how.

Our minds are too complex, but for convenience, let's understand them in a simplified way to solve our issues. Whenever you think or say something, these are not just simple words or thoughts. We are not machines but humans with emotions and feelings. Every word you think or speak is attached to a certain kind of neuron pattern associated with a positive/negative feeling. The mind by its nature attaches keywords with certain feelings.

For example, if one neuron pattern is connected with the word 'thank you', the mind attaches this to the feeling of gratitude. Now, every time you say 'thank you', this neuron pattern will fire up in your mind and a feeling of gratitude will be executed in both your mind and body. Test it now. Just close your eyes, and silently say 'thank you' in your mind to various people you met today. You will feel the undercurrent in your body, a slight pulse of expansion and happiness that you will like.

Now, if you say 'thank you' frequently in your mind or while interacting with others, then this pattern will keep on growing stronger with time. Similarly, when the word 'ill' or 'sick' is repeated and spoken, it is attached to neuron patterns that, when executed, will produce discomfort for you, whether you use the word for yourself or someone else. Repeat this silently, 'I am sick', and you will notice an undercurrent of negativity running through your mind and body. 'Sick' is a frequently used word. Suppose you say this thousands of times, in a span of 2–3 years, you will surely develop certain symptoms the way you conceive your sickness. So, choose your words and sentences wisely in life, they carry a lot of weight. The person who is speaking or thinking about an illness over a long period of time will surely be sick. The mind finally says, 'Your wish will be fulfilled!'

Speaking Your Affirmations Loudly

It takes around 15–20 years for your brain to fully mature.[4] On observing children, we notice that they keep on mumbling sentences and making up stories and talking; so, when we speak aloud and make affirmations, they do have more impact on the mind and new neuron circuits are created. Rather than whispering the affirmations or saying them silently in your head, it is better to say them aloud, whenever possible.

Positive Affirmations

Use positive words. For example, **'I remain calm when speaking to strangers'** is correct, while 'I am not afraid when speaking to strangers' is not.

Fearful language has a way of staying with you. Thus, it's wise to fake it till you make it. Whenever in an affirmation you use the word 'afraid', its corresponding neural pattern gets executed in the brain, which might as well lead you to feel fear instead of banishing it.

Suppose I tell you not to think of a blue rabbit. Then, the first thing you'll think of will be a blue rabbit while trying to ignore it. Similarly, instead of saying, 'I am not feeling uncomfortable', you should say, **'I am feeling comfortable'**.

---

[4]'At What Age is the Brain Fully Developed?', *Mental Health Daily*, 19 February 2015, https://mentalhealthdaily.com/2015/02/18/at-what-age-is-the-brain-fully-developed/. Accessed on 24 May 2023.

Negative Affirmations

Your worst enemy cannot harm you as much
as your own unguarded thoughts.

—The Buddha

Self-deprecation is the biggest crime against yourself. Examples are: I will get sick, my life is short, my memory is getting poorer, I can't do this, this is difficult work, how can I face such a situation, I face trouble everywhere, now what will happen, there is no hope left, situations will worsen, I will meet failure, I am weak, I don't feel comfortable, other people are very clever, I can't travel by air, I can't travel by train as they are filthy…and so on.

The more you repeat such thoughts, the more you are programming your subconscious mind to think more about them. This will lead to a self-fulfilling prophecy.

For example, if you keep being suspicious about your staff or your seniors at work, even if they are honest, you will develop bad relations with them. It is better to move away from people whom you don't trust.

> Don't read negative quotations about anything from anywhere, be it on the internet or from other sources. Try to shift your mindset to believe that life is about experience; when you are happy only then will you be able to experience life; otherwise, your mind will keep on exploiting itself. See life in terms of positive experiences.

Gratitude is the mother of good feelings and you should increase the intensity of your affirmative lines with words like, 'Thank you God for making me the healthiest person.'

Note that the affirmation should be such that it should seem that you have already become happier.

Suppose someone called Rahul has a pet line, 'People in this world are very bad'. He is knowingly/unknowingly repeating this in his mind and he starts feeling irritable with everyone. To counter it, he starts the affirmation, 'Thank you, God, people are very good; they are happy and I feel good interacting with them'. After repeating this many times, his generalized irritation/suspiciousness/phobia about people reduces. Initially, it was very difficult for him to repeat positive affirmations about people because our instinct usually tends to resist a new belief.

Daily Useful Positive Affirmations

I love myself.
I am the healthiest person.
Everyone is very good, everyone is trustworthy.
Go with the flow.
I have a good and sharp memory.
I have the courage to...
Thank you, (name of all the people in school, college, office, people you met today).
With each of the positive affirmations mentioned above, you can say 'Thank you, God', or just 'Thank you' (if you don't believe in a higher power).

VISUALIZATION

Positive affirmations can also be used to mitigate negative feelings. Simultaneously, we can visualize ourselves in a positive situation; for example, enjoying an aeroplane ride instead of fearing taking a flight. Obviously, you will have to practice it for a few days before boarding a flight, and do it daily, so that good feelings can be attached to boarding a flight and travelling by air. The aim is to change the negative construct of flying in our minds and not the actual plane.

Further, feel gratitude towards those who invented planes, who operate them and have made it very convenient for people to travel long distances in a very short span of time.

Remember that visualization doesn't need to be enforced, but creative thinking has to kick in. Whenever you focus on willpower on the spur of the moment to get the results to change, you will not succeed. Since willpower is largely a product of the conscious mind, we need to be relaxed to open up our subconscious minds and feel the visualizations, followed by their implementation.

LETTING GO

The more you let go, the higher you rise.

—Yasmin Mogahed

Let humility be the first defence. If you are stuck in a traffic jam and the situation is out of your control, all you can do is detach your mind from the problem. It seems simple when illustrating the concept of this small problem of traffic. But somehow, we encounter certain troubles in life, which we cannot control sometimes for days or even years. The detachment can only be achieved by attaching a positive feeling to the situation. The more you hate having the problem, the more it will nag you. You need to believe this and find out the logic for yourself. which describes this uncontrollable situation as a positive one. So once again, convert a negative situation through its positive interpretation so that it doesn't disturb your mind.

Just ignoring, avoiding and sidestepping situations does help but does not make you completely positive. There is a need to regularly build a reserve of positive attitude by feeding positive affirmations to your mind daily. Initially, it will require effort, but later on, it will happen naturally.

The art of ignoring is one of the important steps towards mental health. Take the example of an atheist who is watching mythological stories on television where the characters are flying and performing superhuman activities. This person, who believes themselves to be a rational human being, would call these lies. When we become too rigid, we lose the power of being able to ignore. If the mythological character in a TV serial is flying, let it be, take the good lesson out of the story and ignore the rest. If you are giving in to negative emotional responses (like I used to), you keep on reinforcing negative neural patterns in your mind. The more you react, the stronger they become. So, always look into your daily life. You may be doing stupid things and may not realize that you are worsening your mental well-being by keeping prejudices, unnecessary biases, judging people, etc. Ignore and move on and build the capacity to let go.

> We usually say that the issues we cling to in our minds heal with time, but we must be aware that certain things either heal or worsen with time. Thus, it is better to pause and think carefully about every personal issue in life to see how to deal with it.

When you are free from the clutter of prejudices, biases, pre-defined notions and perspectives, your brain has the resources to think and act freely and be more creative. As we age, we usually grow more rigid; thus, our power to ignore and be more creative decreases.

The seven wonders of the world

To see, hear, touch, taste, feel, laugh and love. If you can do these things in life with ease, you are the richest person. Think about those who lack one or more of these sensibilities.

Say, if you are given the option to let go of one organ (your arm or leg) and get five million in exchange, then I hope you will choose your organs. Similarly, to see, hear, touch, taste, feel, laugh and love with a few bucks in the bank are more important than a million bucks without the above. So, take care of your body first.

BE MORE ACCEPTING

Accepting the events in your life can give you peace. With a violent or unacceptable past, you cannot have a peaceful present. Whether you are inflicted with shame, guilt, fear, suppressed emotions, anger or rejection, you need to make peace with it. Accept your unpleasant past by converting it into either positive actions in the present or positively interpreting it; otherwise, it will keep nagging you like the dead villain of Bollywood movies. You cannot escape what has happened, but you need to change yourself to move on in a positive direction. So change now!

Negative events of your past	Positive versions of those events

WHAT IS ACCEPTANCE?

I don't like rain.
I wish it wasn't raining.
My day would be better
if it wasn't raining.
My day is ruined.
Every day is like this now.
It's always like this.
Why does it always rain when
all I want is for it to be sunny?

I accept the rain.
I am not affected by rain.
My day will be fine
irrespective of whether it rains.
Today is going to be a good day!
It doesn't rain every day.
No two days are alike.
Come rain or shine,
I'll enjoy myself.

Say, you have done something wrong that you never wanted to do. Accept that you would not have done it if you knew the consequences. Today, you are wiser than before. Anybody in your position at that time might have done the same or worse than you. Accept your shortcomings in life. Love yourself.

CURIOSITY AND CREATIVITY

Awe and wonder were two great motivations for German-born physicist Albert Einstein. He rejected earlier ways of thinking—looking at nature as other scientists did—and ignored and unlearned old habits and ways. The motive of education should be to know how to think. His passion and curiosity made him the genius we know of today.

When you become passionate and excited about learning again, the formation of dendrites and synapses takes place in the way it happens in children. Being passionate and enthusiastic opens up opportunities for a healthy mind.

Exercise

Put up smiling photographs of personalities, like Einstein, who are a source of creativity and positivity, at your workstation/home etc.

Tip: To stay positive mentally, you have to do what you like or what gives you pleasure almost daily.

Identify and note down the activities that make you happy.

_____

_____

_____

_____

_____

_____

_____

_____

_____

_____

_____

_____

_____

_____

_____

_____

NONE OF THEM CAN READ
BUT SEE THE INTEREST

Do you have a specific purpose in life? To be purposeful is to have hope.

German philosopher Friedrich Nietzsche said, 'He who has a why to live for can bear almost any how.'

You should never run out of plans; you may run out of breath and die, but you should never run out of targets and goals in your life. If you want to live well, live with a concrete target. The brain always wants to work on fascinating and curious projects. It's at work 24×7. Giving it a long-term target makes it busy. As the saying goes, 'An empty mind is the devil's workshop.' However, it would also be appropriate to say, 'An empty mind is Pandora's box of diseases.' Targets should be achievable because not achieving them may be disturbing, though not drastically.

Activities like reading certain articles can help. So, save them on your computer or mobile, and keep cuttings of newspaper articles you like in a folder with the aim that you will write an article that can help others; you can publish them on some websites, answer someone's queries on portals like *Quora* or other social media platforms. This way, you derive a sense of satisfaction from doing social work, which also keeps your mind busy. Or you may opt for long journeys, learn new things from webinars/internet, join some online classes and so on.

[For a list of learning new things, refer to Chapter 12.]

Remember

Doing passionless work is stressful.
Not doing anything is also stressful.

To be happy, you have to pursue either an interest as a hobby or a positive activity, whether physical or not, every day, or at least once in, say, two days. This will constantly reinforce the positive emotional pattern in your mind.

But, what if our mind is playing a trick on us? What if, despite sticking to positive thinking and finding our purpose in life, we are still feeling uncomfortable? Did you know that matters of the mind often manifest through ailments of the body? Let us see how…

5

Mental Health is Physical Too

*The truth never denied the seeker; it is the
seeker who has denied the truth.*

—Robert Tew

Is your mind taking you for a ride? If your answer is 'No', then my next question to you is 'are you as clever as your mind'? You may say yes. But stop. Think again. The mind is cleverer. Our minds do not let us know sometimes what it does. It handles problems without our conscious knowledge, putting our body at risk, but we falsely keep on thinking that the problem lies with other organs, giving us the impression that the mind's own health is fine. Thus, we need to recognize the physical symptoms of mental ailments.

Suppose you are living in a beautiful house and you somehow cannot throw out your house waste. What option will you be left with? Keeping the waste in your living room or bedroom? Obviously, you will say, in the backyard. This happens with your mind too. This is what is meant by being psychosomatic. The word 'psycho' is related to *feeling* and the word 'somatic' is related to the *normal body*. The body and mind work as a unit. Both are interrelated. An effect on one affects the other. This is what we will learn here.

HOW DOES IT WORK?

When tension strikes in the mind (or some resentment, fear, guilt, anxiety, frustration, etc.), the mind subconsciously passes it on to the other parts of the body. It can be a one-time affair or a constant pattern (without your conscious knowledge). It can affect your food pipe or colon, cause tingling or stretching of muscles, put some sort of pressure on your urinary tract, create a hyperactive bladder, sensitive breathing, inflammation, sometimes high blood pressure, palpitation, constipation, farting, stress in the upper or lower portion of legs and leg joints, sometimes cooling your feet, feeling pain on the left side of your chest, a headache, general fatigue despite eating what you normally eat, irritation, etc. This list is not exhaustive. Then, you go to the doctor and they do not find any proper reason why this is happening. It's similar to when you go to a cardiologist after experiencing pain in the left side of your chest. When the doctor says all is well, then you also feel well. Of course, such problems can be genuine too and can be alleviated with appropriate medical attention. But, I would also suggest that you look into other causes; for example, the mind could be unintentionally transferring stress to other body parts.

Let's look at some examples:

1. My close friend, Pankaj, ate curd with the presumption that it was acidic. So, he would have to be cautious while having it regularly. Soon, believing this to be true, he began having symptoms of gastric acidity. As quickly as he had added curd to his diet, he left the same in equal haste. Even then, the feeling of heaviness and acidity was not going away. On

consulting a gastroenterologist, the doctor prescribed some medicines for 2–3 weeks, but still, the acidity did not go away. So, he asked the doctor to conduct an endoscopy, but when the doctor showed him pictures of his gastrointestinal tract, which were normal, Pankaj felt relieved and, in a few minutes, the feeling of acidity vanished and never returned thereafter. He had no medical history of anxiety or stress. So, what was it? Mind games?

2. Before an exam, you may start having pain in the wisdom tooth or a hyperactive bowel syndrome, or urinate frequently. A patient who has undergone some surgery might start manifesting symptoms of pain/itching in/around the surgery area, but when it is examined and diagnosed, everything appears normal.

There are numerous examples I could give here, but let's focus on the main point as, by now, you must have an idea of what all this means.

The mind and body are not like new-age cars, where you attach a computer that will diagnose the glitches and help you to troubleshoot. The mind and body provide symptoms that we usually are unaware of (which we will discuss later in this chapter, along with the solutions) as they are not taught to us when we are young. For that, we need to introspect and retrospect, either with the help of books like this one or professionals. Otherwise, the mind goes into a self-exploitation mode with symptoms of psychosomatic disorders. The system is flashing signals that it needs attention and help but we either don't recognize them or ignore/misdiagnose them.

Psychosomatic disorders can be caused by depression, anxiety, phobias, etc., which lead to or are caused by an imbalance in the chemicals in the brain—decreased serotonin, unbalanced dopamine or increased cortisol. One such affliction is high blood pressure (which is hypertension induced), where the blood vessels contract due to hyperactivity of the SNS and the heart beats fast, leading to an unnatural rise in blood pressure. Blood pressure is generally caused by the deposition of fat in the blood vessels, thereby decreasing the diameter of the vessels. Angina pectoris, the medical term for chest pain, can also be caused by factors of stress. Dermatitis is a general term for skin inflammation, which can also have a psychological origin. Rheumatoid arthritis is an autoimmune disease that can cause joint pain and swelling. Peptic ulcers, ulcerative colitis and irritable bowel syndrome also have one of the co-factors of stress as a trigger.

Note: If you have a history of stress and are taking medication for any of these above diseases, you should also consult your doctor for stress management.

The above-mentioned list is not exhaustive but indicative that these medical issues may happen due to some malfunction in the body along with issues like depression, anxiety, love deprivation, self-deprecation or even stress when you are staying away from your family or when you are overloaded with work. This is when you may resort to excessive smoking or alcohol, which will make your situation even worse in the long run.

What happens is if you have stress, anxiety, fear or resentment in your mind, say, about some person or situation, then you intentionally convince yourself that you are strong or you don't care and think your mind will automatically throw the tension away (without your knowledge). You feel very normal and consider yourself so strong that your anxiety, fear or resentment vanishes, making you think that you have been successful in avoiding stress, but this is usually not the case.

MENTAL HEALTH IS PHYSICAL TOO

The basic concept of psychosomatic disorders was described by Sigmund Freud, who used the term 'conversion hysteria', which means a change in expressive behaviour, i.e. from an unresolved emotion (psychological) to a somatic (physical) symptom.[5]

All this happens because the mind wants to save itself. Rather than throwing bad things out of the body (as it may

---

[5]Ruffalo, Mark L., 'Conversion Disorder: Its History and Implications', *Psychology Today*, 12 June 2018, https://www.psychologytoday.com/us/blog/freud-fluoxetine/201806/conversion-disorder-its-history-and-implications. Accessed on 24 May 2023.

not know how to throw out stress), it converts this into bodily illness and diverts it to other parts of the body.

Exercise

Q: Do you have any chronic illnesses? If yes, do they become worse during stress?

_____

_____

_____

_____

_____

Q: Do stress/situations trigger some chronic illness in you? Have you ever noticed this?

_____

_____

_____

_____

_____

Q: Do you feel shifting pressures in the body, like stretching in the food pipe, which may shift to your legs, then turn into a backache, or manifest in some other form in any other part of your body?

_____

_____

_____

_____

_____

Q: Discuss the above with your near and dear ones.

....

....

....

....

....

....

◆

ANXIETY/FEAR

Fear is targeted towards something, but anxiety engulfs the whole mind and is pervasive.

Anxiety takes a toll on the body in various forms—not eating well or eating excessively, fatigue, heavy respiration, racing heart, acid reflux, erratic sleep, psychosomatic symptoms like chest pain, hyperactive colon or bladder, etc.

Say, for example, Rahul knows that he may fail the exam. He may not be consciously thinking (active memory) about failure, but at the back of his mind, failure is stressing him out (in his passive memory). The back of the mind (subconscious mind) is stressing him without his conscious knowledge.

We must remember that there is an anxiety-attention-memory triangle. With an increase in anxiety, memory decreases.[6] When I used to be under excessive anxiety, I used to forget my ATM password; otherwise, in normal situations, I remembered

---

[6]Grant, DeMond M., and Evan J. White, 'Influence of Anxiety on Cognitive Control Processes', *Oxford Research Encyclopedia of Psychology*, 22 December 2016, https://doi.org/10.1093/acrefore/9780190236557.013.74. Accessed on 24 May 2023.

it with ease. The same is the case with stage fright. When you are conscious and fearful, you forget your lines on stage. So, it is better to visualize and use affirmations before going on stage, or when facing a similar situation in life.

ANXIETY DISORDERS

It is to be noted here that anxiety has its own relevance, it is not always bad. For example, when you are in a dangerous situation, your body and mind switch to fight-or-flight mode—the heart starts beating madly, blood pressure increases and attention increases—so that you can use more resources to tackle the situation. Hence, anxiety becomes functional. But what if it starts getting triggered by small and frivolous events or it remains 'on' constantly? Then, you find yourself in a general anxiety mode, leaving you in a worse situation than before, as you keep putting your body in 'over attention' mode to tackle any dangerous situation. This important mechanism to save our life has now become an obstruction to living your life normally. You have become a movie in which you are the victim of anxiety.

The practical solution is not the motivation or willpower, which will surely wear off after some time. So, let's get down to the solution of cutting down these generalized situations of anxiety. What is the opposite of anxiety? Relaxation. So, use relaxation as the antidote to anxiety.

Our solution to this problem lies in increasing the threshold, i.e. raising the point at which this anxiety is triggered, which can be achieved by practising in such a way that we develop resilience against the frivolous triggering of the SNS that has become hyperactive.

Just close your eyes and say 'relax', and when you repeatedly say this, you will experience a subtle feeling of relaxation throughout your body. You need to attach the feeling of relaxation to the trigger points. As anxiety is generalized, say the word 'relax' along with the name of the person, object or situation (associated with your past, present or future) that is causing you anxiety.

Activity

Let's start the exercise and amend it according to your needs.

- Remember all the faces in your primary class…say their names…after every name say 'relax' whether you liked them or not.
- Do the same with your college friends and acquaintances.
- Now, repeat the exercise for all the people you can think of in your neighbourhood. Do the same for a group.
- Try to find some bad or good situations and after every situation, say 'relax'.

(The word 'relax' should be spoken with the feeling of relaxation so that with every person or situation, you feel relaxed.)

- Now, come to the present situation. Think of a neighbour, office or factory, and then say the word 'relax'. Attach it with material objects, such as a car (driving, tyres, brakes, scooter or clutch) or a mobile (screen or someone calling).
- Then, think about processes. For example, travelling by air, being caught in a wrong situation, office work, exams, etc.

- Remember all your chores one by one, and with each chore say 'relax'.

Your target must be to say the word relax the maximum number of times.

Note down what the specific triggers of your anxiety are with which you must practice; then, you have to practice with everything. You need to make the word 'relax' a keyword. When alone, you can speak it loudly. When walking, with the family or in the office, say it in your mind.

The more you repeat it, even for frivolous things, the less you will need to say it because it will become a general feeling and you will gradually become more relaxed.

Medication is also relevant but the practice of thinking and saying 'relax' will strike the basic thought process, and in time, your personality will change. If you have a high level of anxiety, you must consult medical professionals, but when you need to uproot this evil, this activity needs to be practised religiously along with medical consultation. Some major anxiety disorders are:

1. OCD
2. Social anxiety disorder
3. Panic disorder
4. PTSD
5. Irritability

The form of anxiety can differ from person to person. Is our daughter safe at school? Or, when reading news about theft, you start fearing that burglars would loot your house too. You know you are overthinking and feel nervous but still can't control your thoughts of theft or insecurities concerning your child.

Traps, as we discussed earlier, include high-stress jobs, high expectations and targets, bad or traumatic experiences, underlying inflammations or allergies in the body, having imbalanced diets for a long time or accumulation of bad memories (consciously or unconsciously).

Signs of obsessive-compulsive disorder

OCD refers to the mind obsessively and compulsively thinking about something in a negative way. It leads to activities like unnecessarily washing your hands; thinking anxiously whether you have locked the door; thinking excessively about cleanliness when you observe even a little amount of dirt, which makes you irritated or anxious; excessively finding fault with juniors in office and correcting their grammatical mistakes; obsessively arranging and rearranging household things; or exaggerating certain situations. This way, the mind starts taking you for a ride. This is the beginning, and if not taken care of, it may lead to further deterioration of a person's mental health.

It is understandable when you are worried/anxious about one aspect of life. For example, you become anxious when your parent has some medical issue that you might inherit as you age and this leads to being anxious about everything. You become anxious about driving a car, about the future of your children or grandchildren even if they are well settled, about taking a road trip, when the peon comes and tells you that the boss has asked for you, when you think you are going to miss the train or flight or about an impending exam. Going out of station and living 3-4 days alone takes a toll on you, and you can't eat properly, you have an upset stomach or your hands or other parts of your body are itching or you simply have anxiety.

<u>Important:</u> We need to practice a holistic lifestyle (physical exercise, gratitude, helping others, pursuing hobbies, balanced diet [as discussed in Chapter 6], etc.). Rules of the mind are to be respected and followed; otherwise, nothing will be sustainable.

Signs of social anxiety disorder

A few indications of having social anxiety disorder are stage fright, being in public, becoming conscious of the people around you or unexpected memory lapses while giving a speech, usually in situations where people may be scrutinized, evaluated or judged by others.

Signs of panic disorder

Some signs of having panic disorder are intense fear, heart palpitations or feeling hopelessly out of control, arising out of recurring unexpected panic attacks.

Signs of post-traumatic stress disorder

An attack or assault, a serious accident, a natural disaster, a terrorist attack, being in a war or combat situation or the death of a loved one can trigger post-traumatic stress disorder, either by experiencing the said event or witnessing it.

Signs of irritability

Irritability refers to a tendency to be excited, angry or upset easily. People who are highly irritable are disagreeable and quarrelsome.

Irritability can be generalized; it can even be triggered by short spikes of sound. For example, hearing someone talking loudly on the phone for their lack of common sense or civic sense could give rise to the feeling of 'no one understands me', 'they may land me in trouble' and so on. However, the actual cause of irritability runs deeper, though it expresses itself in these overt forms over small irritants. You know that there's much more to it and it is disturbing your life.

How to Heal Yourself?

Kindness

For inspiration, you can think of Lady Gaga, the famous American singer, songwriter and actress' following words:

> *I've been searching for ways to heal myself,*
> *and I've found that kindness is the best way.*

Laughter

It has been proved that a good laugh can increase blood flow by 15-20 per cent throughout our body.[7] This happens because as we laugh, the inside layer of the blood cells expands and there is a rise in the flow of blood. Watching comedy shows is a good way to do this.

The mind doesn't distinguish between a genuine laugh and a fake one, so celebrate any chance you get to feel happy, like going to the spa, buying a new dress, etc. In fact, buy the smallest and cheapest thing and you will feel happy.

---

[7]Miller, Michael, and William F. Fry, 'The Effect of Mirthful Laughter on the Human Cardiovascular System', *Medical Hypotheses*, Vol. 73, No. 5, 2009, 636–639 https://doi.org/10.1016/j.mehy.2009.02.044.

Make a list of positive people with whom you could talk to

MINIMALISM

Don't pray for worldly gains, just pray for mental peace.

—Anonymous

Let's compare ourselves with our ancestors. As we grow up in today's age, we need to score higher marks than others, get admissions in good schools and colleges, get married, have children, excel to show everyone how happy we are (at least on social media) and have fewer complexities in life. But also, today, we have so many options and the freedom to exercise them. This freedom, however, can also make us sick. When you don't know how to handle it properly, it can also hurt you mentally.

Friends of Aristotle thought that he was satisfied with his frugal life only because he had not exposed himself to the luxuries of the world, so they took him to the market of Athens, which had priceless items. Just when his friends were complacently patting their backs, Aristotle's comment brought them back to earth, 'Oh my god, this world is full of things I don't need!'

Enough of all this mind talk! Can I now interest you in *roti, kapda aur makaan* (food, clothing and shelter, the bare necessities of life)? Or, at least, the first necessity, i.e. food.

6

The Second Brain Feeds the First

Let thy food be thy medicine and medicine be thy food.

—Hippocrates

Our brain is majorly made of fat and water, along with other proteins. All of this produces an incredible consciousness, a living being, and the brain fully depends on our senses of vision, touch, smell, hearing and taste to interpret and experience the world.

Interestingly, the evolution of the brain shows that it has shrunk over a period of time.[8] Nobody knows why. This fact is largely attributed to the loss of fat by way of agricultural dietary habits. In today's modern time, fat has earned a bad name because it clogs our arteries. But, the essential fats—Omega 3 and Omega 6—play complementary roles in the body and the brain. There are certain forms of fats the body cannot manufacture; so, it has to take them from outside through food (such as the Omega 3 fatty acids), which are critical for the body and brain because they have a

---

[8]DeSilva, Jeremy M., James F. A. Traniello, Alexander G. Claxton, and Luke D. Fannin, 'When and Why Did Human Brains Decrease in Size? A New Change-Point Analysis and Insights from Brain Evolution in Ants', *Frontiers in Ecology and Evolution*, Vol. 9, 2021, https://doi.org/10.3389/fevo.2021.742639.

potent anti-inflammatory and antidepressant effect, whereas Omega 6 fatty acids are largely inflammatory by nature. Anthropologists have found that our ancestors had a larger intake of Omega 3 fatty acids, and these are found in various nuts, seeds, vegetables and fish.

When there is a lack of Omega 3 in the brain, serotonin—the happy hormone—is not able to function properly because the cells need to understand the messages that are being passed. According to recent studies, our ancestors had Omega 3 and Omega 6 in the ratio of 1:1 in their bodies. When human beings settled down, from being nomadic hunter-gatherers to a life based on agriculture, the above ratio reached 1:5, which has now become lopsided at 1:15 in Western diets.[9] It is being researched that the imbalance in the ratios of Omega 3 to Omega 6 is the cause of chronic inflammation (and autoimmune diseases) in the human body and for some, the dietary imbalance leads to depression, while for others, it may lead to other diseases depending upon their body types.

Sources of Omega 3 fats: Grass, algae and plant leaves.

Sources of Omega 6 fats: Mostly found in plant seeds. They are abundant in grains and nuts, which are technically seeds. Examples include soya beans, corn, sunflower seeds, etc.

The Japanese have a good ratio of Omega 3 and Omega 6 because they have incorporated sea fish into their daily diet.

---

[9]Gunnars, Kris, 'How to Optimize Your Omega-6 to Omega-3 Ratio', *Healthline*, 15 February 2023, https://www.healthline.com/nutrition/optimize-omega-6-omega-3-ratio. Accessed on 25 May 2023.

Start taking Vitamin C regularly because it helps protect Omega 3 by reducing oxidative stress.

Giving a high dose of Vitamin D to certain patients is also known to have an uplifting effect on their mood. Vitamin D has anti-inflammatory and immune-modulating properties, i.e. it can make the immune system work in tandem with the body.[10]

Vitamin D deficiency was never an issue with our ancestors because they were spending most of their time in the sun. Also, when early man settled for farming, then too much exposure to sunlight was normal in comparison to today's exposure to sunlight as we usually stay inside offices or houses during daytime. Not being exposed to the sun reduces the efficacy of body cells to produce Vitamin D.

Vitamin D contains Vitamins D2 and D3. We need Vitamin D3, which is produced by our body when it is exposed to sunlight. We obtain many nutrients from milk, and Vitamin D2 is one of them, but it is not the same as that which is produced by our body.

---

[10]Rodriguez, Alexander J., Aya Mousa, Peter R. Ebeling, David Scott, and Barbora de Courten, 'Effects of Vitamin D Supplementation on Inflammatory Markers in Heart Failure: A Systematic Review and Meta-Analysis of Randomized Controlled Trials', *Scientific Reports*, Vol. 8, 2018, 1169. https://doi.org/10.1038/s41598-018-19708-0.

FOOD FOR THE 'BRAIN'

No guts no glory, no legend no story.

—Anonymous

We will be continuing our discussion on 'food for thought' or 'food for the mind', but with a twist. Our body is an ecosystem, which is also the living space for our gut flora.

Our gastrointestinal system (gut) is a group of organs, including the mouth, oesophagus, stomach, pancreas, liver, gall bladder, small intestine, colon (large intestine) and rectum. Now, the gut flora is the microbiome consisting of bacteria, protozoa and viruses that live within our guts and act as our companions. In contrast, the vagus nerves represent the main component of the PNS and oversee crucial bodily functions, including mood regulation, immune response, digestion and heart rate. The gut flora is a powerful being that regulates our second brain and can still work with its own 'mind' and perform functions independently, even when the vagus nerves are injured/severed. The gut is a neural channel, i.e. it has more neurons than the spinal cord itself. The gut microbiome consists of thousands of species, and is like our fingerprints, where every human has a different set of microbes.[11] This gastrointestinal tract is supposed to have its own intelligence and these living beings in our guts determine our lives and

---

[11]Tomasello, Giovanni, Margherita Mazzola, Abdo Jurjus, Francesco Cappello, Francesco Carini, Provvidenza Damiani, Alice Gerges Geagea, Zeenny M.N., and Angelo Leone, 'The Fingerprint of the Human Gastrointestinal Tract Microbiota: A Hypothesis of Molecular Mapping', *Journal of Biological Regulators and Homeostatic Agents*, Vol. 31, No. 1, 2017, 245–249. https://pubmed.ncbi.nlm.nih.gov/28337900/.

destinies by way of controlling and affecting our emotions and health of the mind.

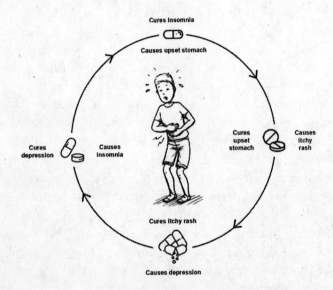

Cures insomnia

Causes upset stomach

Cures upset stomach

Causes itchy rash

Cures depression

Causes insomnia

Cures itchy rash

Causes depression

New research indicates a mutual relationship between gut health and mental health.[12] This gut–brain axis has always been underrated, and only now it is getting its due importance.

The digestive system is regulated by the nervous system, which is made up of around 500 million nerve cells and is regulated by the same neurotransmitters as the brain.

---

[12]Shoubridge, Andrew P., Jocelyn M. Choo, Alyce M. Martin, Damien J. Keating, Ma-Li Wong, Julio Licinio, and Geraint B. Rogers, 'The Gut Microbiome and Mental Health: Advances in Research and Emerging Priorities', *Molecular Psychiatry*, Vol. 27, 2022, 1908–1919. https://doi.org/10.1038/s41380-022-01479-w.

Serotonin (along with other required chemicals) is produced in the stomach, which is why it is also called the second brain. The stomach has a muscular wall that contains around 35 million gastric glands that secrete around three litres of juices in a day.

FUNCTIONS OF THE 'SECOND BRAIN' (GUT)

The importance of microbes lies in their crucial role to allow the absorption of nutrients from food. The issue is not how much we eat but how many absorbable nutrients are available in the food we eat. As we are becoming more health and diet conscious, we are eating nutrient-dense diets, but what if our gut microbes don't act on the eaten food and the required nutrients aren't absorbed?

If there is an issue in absorbing nutrients because of some gastrointestinal issue or the thyroid tissue, it means our body has fallen out of balance and becomes vulnerable to some known or unknown inflammation, thus activating the emotional part of the brain.

Some believe that the Roman civilization died because of the construction of lead-lined aqueducts, which were toxic, as the human immune system is unable to fight lead. What if we are consuming extremely slow poisons in our food today?

Millions of neurons and nerves run between our brain and gut. Neurotransmitters and other chemicals formed in our guts also affect our brains. By altering the types of bacteria in our guts, it may be possible to improve our brain's health.

The microbes in our guts teach the immune system how to defeat the harmful microorganisms entering our bodies.

Researchers are at the initial stages of studying the complex relationship between microbiomes and immunity.[13] Harmful microorganisms enter the body and colonize the gut, but are kept in check by the friendly gut microbes. A proper understanding of this is going to have great implications in finding solutions to chronic diseases, such as Crohn's, ulcerative colitis and irritable bowel syndrome, in which the immune system starts fighting against your body parts.

Gut microbes are the little drug factories that are producing biochemicals having *antidepressant and anti-anxiety effects*, thereby affecting our brain. Much of the serotonin, a natural antidepressant neurotransmitter, is produced in the gut. From this, it becomes clear that the gut has a crucial role in determining our state of happiness and unhappiness and thus, our mind's health.

Lactobacillus and *Bifidobacterium* microbes in the gut produce gamma-aminobutyric acid (GABA), our main inhibitory neurotransmitter, which has a relaxing effect on our minds and bodies, thereby relieving anxiety.[14]

The microbes *Bacillus* and *Serratia* in the gut are the producers of the motivational neurotransmitter dopamine.[15] *Bifidobacterium*

[13]Zheng, Danping, Timur Liwinski, and Eran Elinav, 'Interaction between Microbiota and Immunity in Health and Disease', *Cell Research*, Vol. 30, 2020, 492–506. https://doi.org/10.1038/s41422-020-0332-7.

[14]Barros-Santos, Thaísa, Kallyane Santos Oliveira Silva, Matheus Libarino-Santos, Elisangela Gouveia Cata-Preta, Henrique Sousa Reis, Eduardo Koji Tamura, Alexandre Justo de Oliveira-Lima, Laís Fernanda Berro, Ana Paula Trovatti Uetanabaro, and Eduardo Ary Villela Marinho, 'Effects of Chronic Treatment with New Strains of *Lactobacillus plantarum* on Cognitive, Anxiety- and Depressive-Like Behaviors in Male Mice', *PLoS One*, Vol. 15, No. 6, 2020, e0234037. https://doi.org/10.1371/journal.pone.0234037.

[15]Strandwitz, Philip, 'Neurotransmitter Modulation by the Gut Microbiota',

infantis, which is a probiotic, has an antidepressant effect on a par with the anti-anxiety drug citalopram.

Now, it is not surprising to know that the personality of an individual is shaped by gut microbes. It's quite natural that whatever affects our mind—including the biochemicals (along with others) produced in the gut—shapes the way we feel and think. Therefore, it's expected that the gut is called the second brain. Ninety per cent of the visceral nerve carries information from the gut to the brain, where it is interpreted as emotions.[16]

In a case study of a faecal transplant from a healthy but fat daughter to a lean mother for treating *Clostridium difficile* infection (whose symptoms included diarrhoea, stomach pain and fever), some interesting results became evident.[17] After certain weeks of gestation in the mother, her personality changed. She put on weight, like her daughter, despite exercises and physical activities and other methods to restrain the increase in weight. This study exhibits the astounding effect of microbiomes on shaping a person's body and outlook.

A caesarean section or C-section is the surgical method of delivering a baby through incisions in the abdomen and

Brain Research, Vol. 1693, Part B, 2018, 128–133. https://doi.org/10.1016/j.brainres.2018.03.015.

[16]Rosenfeld, Jordan, '10 Smart Facts About Your Gut', *Mental Floss*, 9 October 2018, https://www.mentalfloss.com/article/64685/10-brainy-facts-about-your-gut-its-smarter-you-think. Accessed on 12 May 2023.

[17]Gallagher, James, 'Woman's Stool Transplant Leads to "Tremendous Weight Gain"', *BBC News*, 7 February 2015, https://www.bbc.com/news/health-31168511. Accessed on 12 May 2023. **Faecal transplant** involves transplanting faeces from a healthy donor into another person to restore the balance of bacteria in their gut in order to help treat gastrointestinal infections and other conditions.

uterus. It has been found that in the mother's birth canal, there is a coating of bacteria that is passed on to the newborn when the birthing is natural. However, in a caesarean section, the baby does not come in contact with the mother's microbiome and a child born through this method is more prone to physical and mental ailments.[18]

In various tests conducted on mice, it has been found that those having diverse microbes in the gut were more active, but those with a weak gut showed anxious and depressive behaviour. Not only this, when the *Toxoplasma gondii* (protozoan parasite that infects most species of warm-blooded animals) microbe was transplanted and colonized in rodents, they lost their fear of cats and instead got attracted towards them. This illustrates that the fear factor was being regulated by certain neurotransmitters produced by the *Toxoplasma gondii* microbe.[19]

New research is pointing to certain underlying factors behind autism in children, but nothing concrete has emerged thus far. There are, however, indications that it is the *health and diversity* of microbiomes that have an impact on autism.[20] The majority of kids with autism suffer from gastrointestinal problems. Various medical case study reports underline the fact that a child with autism is exposed to antibiotics for some

---

[18]Gallagher, James, 'Vaginal Birth and Caesarean: Differences in Babies' Bacteria', *BBC News*, 18 September 2019, https://www.bbc.com/news/health-49740735. Accessed on 12 May 2023.

[19]Barford, Eliot, 'Parasite Makes Mice Lose Fear of Cats Permanently', *Nature*, 18 September 2013, https://doi.org/10.1038/nature.2013.13777. Accessed on 12 May 2023.

[20]Kotsiliti, Eleni, 'Gut Microbiome and Autism Spectrum Disorder', *Nature Reviews Gastroenterology & Hepatology*, Vol. 19, 2021, 6. https://doi.org/10.1038/s41575-021-00564-9.

ailment or the other, such as a respiratory issue, quite early on in their life.[21] The antibiotics not only destroy the bad microbes but also the friendly ones, and are therefore a threat to the friendly biomes inside our guts. **Losing microbes is just like losing an organ of the body.** So it won't be wrong to say that if we don't find better substitutes for antibiotics, then our future generations are going to have serious issues related to mental health.

IMPORTANCE OF THE GUT

How Can We Change Our Eating Habits?

We have waged a war against bacteria by creating various antibiotics that not only kill harmful microbes but also devastate the friendly microbes in our guts. Our food civilization is tilted towards fibreless food, refined carbohydrates and sugars. *The dietary fibrous food that we have given up for processed food is actually not just a question of our diet but the diet of our companion microbiota living in our guts.* The health of the body and mind depends on the health and diversity of microbiota. Not eating fibrous food, which is food for the microbiomes in our body, has ramifications for our mental well-being. Food that is healthy for the gut is like taking food as medicine.[22] Therefore, better

---

[21]Łukasik, Jan, Bernadeta Patro-Gołąb, Andrea Horvath, Ruth Baron, Hania Szajewska, and the SAWANTI Working Group, 'Early Life Exposure to Antibiotics and Autism Spectrum Disorders: A Systematic Review', *Journal of Autism and Developmental Disorders*, Vol. 49, 2019, 3866–3876. https://doi.org/10.1007%2Fs10803-019-04093-y.

[22]Olayanju, Julia B., 'Food as Medicine: Understanding the Importance of Food to Gut Health', *Forbes*, 21 August 2019, https://www.forbes.com/

eating habits will ensure that the microbiota and our body and mind's health stay in harmony.

Natural and artificial probiotics come in handy, which are the compounds that induce the growth of helpful microorganisms in the gut. Secondly, probiotics are live bacteria and yeast, which are taken for diversifying and promoting the growth of gut microbiomes.

Probiotic foods: Whole foods, such as fruits, whole grains and vegetables, can lead to diverse gut flora. Fermented foods (yoghurt, kimchi, sauerkraut, kefir, kombucha and tempeh) are the best sources of probiotics.

Anti-gut bacteria biodiversity: Alcohol, imbalanced sleep, disturbed circadian rhythm, too much stress, antibiotics and staying on a diet containing one or two kinds of food grains, especially wheat and rice.

New Trends

Although today our bodies are almost the same as those of our ancestors, modern-day lifestyle threats are entirely different. Our ancestors' immune system was designed through evolution to fight against limited chemical and microbe diversity, and the immune system could identify and destroy the enemies that were known to it, but today, the situation has changed drastically. Nowadays, there are superbugs with anti-bacterial microbial resistance to anti-bacterial medicines and toxic chemicals, which include pesticides, insecticides, fertilizers, plastics and genetically modified and hybridized foods.

---

sites/juliabolayanju/2019/08/21/food-as-medicine--understanding-the-importance-of-food-to-gut-health/. Accessed on 26 May 2023.

Is Sugar Bad for the Intestines?

Fructose (commercially derived from sugar cane, sugar beets and maize) stays in the gut, causing gastrointestinal bloating and uneasiness. It also interferes with the absorption of nutrients and water in the larger intestine, i.e. colon.

How Do You Clean Out Your Gut?

Eating diverse and fibre-rich foods helps in restoring the diversity of your gut bacteria. Use antibiotics only when they are absolutely required. Further, exercising daily and drinking plenty of water works wonders for your gut.

Quality of Stools

The bowel transit time depends upon how active you are. For an average man, it can be 55–60 hours, but for a woman, it can be up to 72 hours.

Every meal we consume goes into the stomach and then the small intestine before it enters the larger intestine (colon), where it can be stored for up to 2–3 days. The colon is a large fermentation tank, where billions of bacteria act upon the fibre we have consumed and try to extract the nutrients for the body before discarding the rest.

For reasons still not understood by researchers, a happy colon means a reduction in the risk of diabetes, cancers, heart disease, depression, and all kinds of anxiety.

Every gram of wet faeces we produce contains around 100 billion bacteria and 100 million archaea (bacteria-like microbes that can inhabit some of the most extreme environments on Earth such as hot springs, deep sea vents or extremely acidic waters).[23] An analysis of the samples can also reveal many amoebas, fungi, bacteriophages, alveolates and basidiomycetes.

STOOL FORMATION

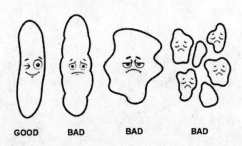

GOOD   BAD   BAD   BAD

In a small study, researchers compared stool samples from two groups of children—children with autism having gastrointestinal symptoms and those without autism and gastrointestinal symptoms. The researchers identified significantly higher amounts of *Clostridium perfringens* bacteria in samples collected from autistic children with gastrointestinal symptoms.[24]

Leaky Gut Syndrome

Leaky gut is a condition of gastric permeability in which the lining of the small intestine becomes ruptured, resulting in

---

[23]Ho, Vincent, 'Your Poo is (Mostly) Alive. Here's What's in It', *The Conversation*, 31 October 2018, https://theconversation.com/your-poo-is-mostly-alive-heres-whats-in-it-102848. Accessed on 12 May 2023.

[24]How the Gut Microbiome Affects the Brain and Mind, YouTube, https://www.youtube.com/watch?v=b4CBy0uVqRc. Accessed on 12 May 2023.

the food particles of undigested food or bacteria directly entering the bloodstream. Many professionals don't acknowledge leaky gut syndrome as a diagnosable condition. As you now know, the gastrointestinal tract is home to an extensive range of microbes. These support digestion, facilitate the immune system and protect the intestinal wall, and most importantly, produce the happy hormone serotonin, dopamine and other hormones responsible for good psychological health. It is important to note that the antidepressant and anti-happy hormones are produced by *Candida*, *Streptococcus* and *Escherichia*. It is to be noted that day-to-day brain health and cognition are affected by the gut microbe's performance.

An imbalance in gut biodiversity may result in inflammation of the smaller or larger intestine, which may not be diagnosed. That's why some researchers call it a silent killer.

A leaky gut may lead to:

- Irritable bowel syndrome
- Crohn's disease
- Proctitis
- Ulcerative colitis
- Celiac disease
- Chronic liver disease
- Diabetes
- Polycystic ovary syndrome
- Food allergy

Mental conditions, such as depression and anxiety, are also linked to what is called the gut–brain arc. Researchers are still probing whether leaky gut syndrome is the syndrome or the cause of these conditions.

DID YOU SAY LACTOSE INTOLERANT?

We have eulogized milk so much that it has become an inseparable part of our diets. It has become like a custom or ritual to have milk at least once every day. But have you ever given serious thought to the fact that the milk we are consuming is actually meant for cow or buffalo calves? Is the milk that is supposed to increase the calf's weight from 2.5 to 3.5 kg per day suitable for us? Do human children or adults also need such weight or do they have digestive machinery similar to that of calves? Children or infants do have lactase enzymes to break up milk nutrients but, as we grow, the production of this enzyme slows down.[25] Because of low production of lactase, irritation and other side effects develop in the smaller or larger intestine. According to one estimate, about 68 per cent of the world's population is lactose intolerant.[26]

Dairy protein can be classified into two proteins, namely, whey and casein protein. Milk contains around 80 per cent casein protein and 20 per cent whey protein wherein one is a fast-digesting protein but the other takes time. This protein can trigger inflammation and pain in the joints. You can only test this by not having dairy products for 2–3 weeks and observing how it affects your general health.

Dairy allergies are common in people of all ages. However, as the allergy levels are generally low, it becomes difficult to

[25]'Lactose Intolerance,' *Mayo Clinic*, 5 March 2022, https://www.mayoclinic. org/diseases-conditions/lactose-intolerance/symptoms-causes/syc-20374232. Accessed on 26 May 2023.

[26]'Definition & Facts for Lactose Intolerance,' *National Institute of Diabetes and Digestive and Kidney Diseases*, https://www.niddk.nih.gov/ health-information/digestive-diseases/lactose-intolerance/definition-facts. Accessed on 12 May 2023.

self-diagnose. This everyday allergy may lead to chronic auto-immune diseases in the future, the effect of which you may not even realize all your life.

> Milk may also take up to 2–4 days to show symptoms like bloating, indigestion, itching in the rectum, leaky gut, improper formation of stools, diarrhoea and constant constipation.

> The Amish communities in America have a low rate of depression as they follow a healthy lifestyle, living on the same diet that dates back to the eighteenth century.[27]
>
> Further, the lifestyle of the Kaluli people of the New Guinea Highlands, who are a part of the hunting and gathering societies even now, results in almost zero rates of depression or other mental health ailments.[28]

THEN THERE'S GLUTEN SENSITIVITY

The book *Toxic Staple*[29] recounts stories of people who recovered from various ailments, such as acid reflux, allergies and even complicated neurological problems, by somehow

---

[27]Lantz, Gregory, *Perceptions of Lifestyle as Mental Health Protective Factors Among Midwestern Amish*, 2019. Walden University, PhD dissertation. https://scholarworks.waldenu.edu/cgi/viewcontent.cgi?article=8963&context=dissertations.

[28]Omega Recovery Treatment Center, 'Our Mental Health Crisis as a Cultural Phenomenon', *Omega Recovery*, 12 April 2018, https://omegarecovery.org/our-mental-health-crisis-as-a-cultural-phenomenon/. Accessed on 29 May 2023.

[29]Sarkisian, Anne, *Toxic Staple: How Gluten May Be Wrecking Your Health and What You Can Do About It!*, Max Health Press, New London, New Hampshire, 30 September 2013.

restraining from the consumption of wheat as they were gluten sensitive.

Here is an interesting study by the Dutch paediatrician Dr Willem-Karel Dicke who was working on issues related to celiac disease. Towards the end of the years 1944 and 1945, i.e. when the Second World War was coming to an end, there was a winter of starvation, a dearth of bread and amazingly, it was noticed that children who had celiac disease got better. But, when the supply of bread picked up again, the symptoms of the disease started manifesting once more.[30]

Within the lining of the gastrointestinal system, there are spaces between the cells of the intestine, which are like tight junctions as they remain closed and open only at appropriate times. According to a discovery by Dr Alessio Fasano in 2000 at the University of Maryland, a protein called zonulin triggered the walls of the gut to open and allowed the gluten protein found in wheat, rye and barley to escape directly into the bloodstream, thereby causing autoimmune diseases.[31] The more dangerous part is that the wheat we are consuming right now belongs to the high yielding varieties of the Green Revolution and has a substantially higher level of gluten content as compared to the wheat varieties that our ancestors were consuming. Hence, our bodies have become more prone to autoimmune issues, chronic inflammation, etc.

---

[30]Messier, Gilles, 'How a WWII Famine Helped Solve a 2,000 Year Old Major Medical Mystery', *Today I Found Out*, 17 June 2022, https://www.todayifoundout.com/index.php/2022/06/how-a-wwii-famine-helped-solve-a-2000-year-old-major-medical-mystery/. Accessed on 12 May 2023.

[31]Barlow, Ellen, 'Celiac Disease and the Unforeseen Path to Discovery', *Celiac Disease Foundation*, 8 December 2014, https://celiac.org/about-the-foundation/featured-news/2014/12/celiac-disease-unforeseen-path-discovery/. Accessed on 29 May 2023.

According to an estimate, 80–90 per cent of gluten sensitivity problems remain undiagnosed, and this is a major trigger for chronic and autoimmune diseases in the body, even if you are trying to lead a healthy lifestyle.[32] Dr Fasano calls wheat sensitivity a chameleon, ranging from chronic diseases to chronic diarrhoea, weight loss and even organ failures like cardiac arrest.[33]

Wheat is also related to a spike in energy (its glycaemic index is high) because it contains more carbohydrates, and thus may lead to insulin resistance over a longer period of time, increased inflammation and weight gain. This may not only happen to people who have celiac disease but to others as well.

> Hunger-induced anger (or being hangry) occurs when glucose levels in the blood drop, which is treated as a life-threatening situation triggering the fight-or-flight response in the body.

> When we are dehydrated, our energy levels drop significantly. This drop in energy causes our minds to crave sugar but actually, dehydration is making our bodies crave water. The signal for needing water is often misinterpreted as a craving for sugar; thus, especially in the case of older people, dehydration leads to cognitive confusion. Therefore, staying hydrated is a key solution to lowering our sugar

[32]Patrick, Sarah, '7 Serious Complications of Untreated Celiac Disease', *Gluten Intolerance School*, 8 April 2021, https://glutenintoleranceschool.com/7-serious-complications-of-untreated-celiac-disease/. Accessed on 29 May 2023.

[33]Celiac Disease and Non-Celiac Gluten Sensitivity: Is There a Difference? Alessio Fasano, MD, YouTube, https://www.youtube.com/watch?v=flBtI84tJNE. Accessed on 12 May 2023.

cravings. When we feel the need, we should drink water and stay hydrated. The tragedy of our time is that we have been brainwashed that sugar is necessary for us; so, instead of getting it from refined sources, it's better to do so from fruits and vegetables, especially when they are eaten raw. Also, juices available in the market should be avoided as they contain high amounts of added sugars. Even the juices made at home will not serve much purpose; it is better that fruits are eaten in their natural form along with fibre.

While food for the first brain (our brain) and second brain (our gut) balances the system (our body), the system also needs its balanced diet to stay healthy. But, in this age of unlimited options and an abundance of junk food, how to choose what's best to satiate the body?

7

Eat Well to Stay Well

When food is wrong, medicine is of no use.
When food is right, medicine is of no need.

—Dr Khadar Vali

What you are about to read now is more important than what you have read so far in this book. Changing your diet is a fundamental issue, which will help you bring about a sustainable change in your life. You have to eat well in order to stay well.

When your health starts to suffer, you seek a doctor for remedies and start taking the prescribed pills and feel alright, until you stop your medicines and find yourself in the same situation as before. Bringing small changes in lifestyle can help but they are not enough for restoring your body to optimal health. This is also the crux of my story shared below.

Back in 2002, I noticed blood in my stool. I was diagnosed with ulcerative colitis (a condition that causes inflammation and ulcers [sores] in the digestive tract). I was prescribed Mesacol, which I took from time to time. I should have understood the message my body was trying to send across then, that I needed to make a major change in my lifestyle; however, I did not know what to do. No one in my family has had ulcerative colitis.

During 2003–2007, I got into college. I was good at studies but destiny had its own plan. At that time, my attention was focussed on my romantic prospects in a one-sided relationship. Therefore, I could not perform well in my exams. I was greatly impacted by this and could barely manage myself. I could not answer why I was in this one-sided relationship despite knowing that I had to focus on my studies. I had to wait until 2017–2018 to realize that it was indeed a sign of how I was drifting towards depression and anxiety. Fortunately, I managed to graduate on time. However, while preparing for the civil services exam in June 2009, I was diagnosed with depression and general anxiety disorder. The diagnosis was, however, a tricky one. The cause in my case was that I couldn't eat anything because of a choking sensation, for which I was consulting the same gastroenterologist who was treating me for ulcerative colitis. I didn't feel any kind of stress/tension, but I was somewhat anxious and frustrated. The doctor gave me antacids and other relaxants and advised me to take an appointment with a psychiatrist. He suspected that the underlying cause wasn't gastrointestinal, rather it was related to anxiety and depression. I still remember arguing with my doctor. I kept saying I had no stress, but he did not budge from his position, and that's how my new journey started, albeit not of my volition (as is the case with everyone). I was prescribed a heavy dose of medicines, slept for long hours and suffered from muscle aches and chronic fatigue, yet there was not much relief. I was taking medicines for ulcerative colitis, anxiety and depression on and off, but their positive impact was too slow. Over the years, I have been on different medications at different stages of my treatment, and though they could not provide much relief, I was able to carry out my daily chores because of them.

Then, in 2019, I was put on paroxetine, a kind of SSRI, which was an eye-opener for me as it worked really well. I felt the same childlike energy I used to have. I felt as though my life had become beautiful again. My doctor told me to continue taking paroxetine for 8–12 months, and it was subsequently tapered off. Everything seemed fine until six months later, in 2020, when my wellness bubble burst and I was back in the same alley of anxiety and depression. It was probably because of the depleting serotonin reservoir in my body that was being created and maintained by paroxetine earlier.

Although I could have started the same medicine as before, I was adamant about reclaiming my health without medicine this time. This is how my quest with different kinds of foods began, thereby paving the way for sustainable change primarily through various types of food.

The first thing we need to do to regain wellness is to change our habits, like start eating dry fruits, drinking warm water in the morning on an empty stomach or exercising to detox the body. Our mind's health is connected to that of the gut. Therefore, any sustainable change has to begin from here, i.e. the gut. If someone tells you that it's all in your head and you need to control your thoughts and feel happy, that is not completely true.

LIFESTYLE CHANGES AND ASSOCIATED ISSUES

Dietary changes improve mental health by resolving issues in the gut. So, it is best to have control over what we eat. Trust your instincts and observe symptoms, if any, and take cues from these to become aware of your body and health. Connect the dots. Try to find out what makes you uneasy and see which diet has a negative and positive impact on you.

So, when should you experiment? When you can tell that your health is slowly deteriorating due to anxiety, depression, OCD, high/low blood pressure, acid reflux, high pulse rate, chronic fatigue, etc., it's time to experiment with diets. However, if you are on prescribed medicines or still showing symptoms despite being on medication, you won't be able to determine what food is affecting you. (Don't skip your prescribed medicines to test diets.)

> **Caution:** As is the case with changing seasons, we must change our diet with age. As you age, you can't expect your body to digest the same food that you were eating at the ages of 8, 28 or 38. Therefore, experimenting with food may serve you well as you age. If you don't do so, your body may show various symptoms, which may vary from person to person. For example, if you continue to be on a high carbohydrate diet, then you may run the risk of diabetes or other complications.

As part of my experiment with food in 2020, I started eating maize dishes instead of wheat for two weeks. I could sense a subtle change in my feel-good factor. However, again, I ate wheat dishes, and it took only one week to start feeling subtle waves of anxiety, especially before going to sleep. So, I switched back to maize for the next 3–4 days, and I could tell that there was a considerable drop in my anxiety. But, to be sure, I repeated this experiment around five times, replacing wheat with maize, and only then it became clear that wheat was somehow triggering my anxiety. I subsequently went for a blood test for gluten sensitivity but the result was negative. However, my instincts were pointing towards an incompatibility with wheat. A biopsy is usually recommended for wheat allergy or celiac disease. There is also non-celiac gluten sensitivity, which has a direct link with mental, emotional and neurological disorders. Unfortunately, I could not get the test done due to accessibility issues. I cut down my wheat intake anyway. The switch to maize was not easy since it tends to be a bit rough and non-sticky and has little to offer in terms of taste. So occasionally, I ate wheat chapatis. This did not go well though.

My capacity to eat wheat (which I was already eating less) was decreasing drastically day by day. Just after eating 2–3 wheat chapatis, my heart rate used to shoot up (a symptom of anxiety). I was prescribed clonazepam for this. Now, I had no other option except to abruptly stop eating wheat and look for an alternative to maize (a note of caution: do not abandon wheat all at once as you may then suffer from acute uneasiness). I had no option but to start eating jowar (sorghum) chapati. However, this too wasn't a wise decision. One night, I ate around 3–4 chapatis with curry and went to sleep. Around midnight, I felt uneasy and took this to be a symptom of anxiety and seizure. Fortunately, my friend was staying with me that night. My instincts were craving sugar, salt, bananas and noodles. After 15–20 minutes, I also took an SOS tablet prescribed by the doctor and went back to sleep. Jowar has a low glycaemic index than wheat and was not providing me with an adequate level of carbohydrates. Thereafter, I faced the same situation more than 3–4 times until I settled down with a proper diet.

Caution: Never stop eating food that is high in carbohydrates abruptly. It may give your severe withdrawal symptoms. As your body is in the habit of eating more carbs, inadequate levels of carbohydrates can cause uneasiness, low sugar levels, high heart rate or low blood pressure, headaches, etc. It may take 20-30 days to switch to a low-carb diet along with uneasiness. It's always better to taper off wheat over 3-4 months.

> Further, avoid jau flour (barley) because it too contains gluten.

For me, bananas became a great substitute for wheat; it helped me maintain my carbohydrate levels.

> **Tip:** If you want to switch to a low-carb diet, make sure you cut down on your intake during day time; doing this during dinner, before going to sleep, may lead to a drop in your sugar levels, causing you trouble in mid-sleep. This is because there is a long gap between dinner and breakfast.

By July 2020, I had stopped eating wheat completely. By the first week of August, the feeling of depression was gone, although the anxiety issue continued to linger. Those who wish to drop wheat from their diet can first use a mixture of wheat, ragi, jowar flour plus millet (how to use millets is provided in the following text), and then taper off wheat gradually.

Now, you may say that you can't suffer from wheat allergy and leaving it won't make you feel better. Even I used to consider wheat as normal as its symptoms were so mild that my body was fighting with it for the last 3–4 years without my conscious knowledge. It was only lately that I realized that my body's wheat tolerance had dropped drastically. What if my body showed signs of poor wheat tolerance and I could not comprehend them? Can wheat intolerance trigger symptoms of depression? Well, there is no harm in trying an alternative for four weeks and then reaching a conclusion.

As discussed earlier, the SNS must have kicked in either due to stress or eating pro-anxiety foods, thereby accelerating the heart rate. I could not identify the nefarious work of wheat earlier, but now, its effect became clear.

Cucumber intake: In 2017, I was experimenting with different salads; I had started eating one or two cucumbers post lunch every day. After a couple of days or so, just after waking up in the morning, I felt that I had lost weight as I was feeling too light. I checked my weight on the machine and got a normal reading. However, after 2-3 days, I stopped eating cucumber and I started feeling heavy again. I repeated this experiment many times and realized that cucumber was working for me. As we will read further, cucumber was settling Pitta dosha (as described in Ayurveda) in me; along with retainable water too. Till date, I make sure I eat fruits, including cucumber.

The next issue was my heart rate; whenever an acute anxiety episode started (2–3 episodes every day), it triggered heart palpitations. I found a simple way to fix this: by eating seasonal fruits every day. Say you weigh 80 kg, so make sure you eat 800 grams of fruit every day. Do not compromise on this. This way, dehydration (which you may not consciously feel) is tackled, and you get numerous vitamins, minerals and antioxidants. The very intake of fruits every day helped me in stabilizing my irregular heartbeat. I can only guess why my anxiety was suo moto or due to other petty reasons like a disturbing event in the office or something similar. The reason I found was just dehydration. All my life I have been eating dry chapatis, but my body was asking for hydration, and this hydration is not possible with normal water intake, but with fruits i.e. fibre and water both in the same diet.

Just drinking water is not the best way to stay hydrated. When you urinate, you may be losing important salts. This may cause an electrolyte imbalance, which may lead to further health issues if dehydration is not properly addressed for a long period of time. So, it's better to eat fruits than to drink gallons of water.

During monsoons, we need to be cautious while eating fruits. So, how should we go about it? We must peel the skin of the fruit; this way we will be able to avoid pesticides/insecticides and, most importantly, pathogens. Food poisoning from an infected fruit can mess up our stomach for 7–15 days. So, better peel off the skin to avoid any complications.

> I used to feel pressure on my nose but didn't know what to make of it. Now, I have realized the root cause. It is dehydration, and simply consuming water is not enough. We must eat fresh fruits for at least one or two days every week.
> Everybody has different symptoms, so you must introspect.

There was another issue I had been facing for a while. I was feeling a pinched nerve pain in my neck; it used to rise and subside, but I had no idea why this was happening. I was looking for solutions when one day I remembered what an ayurvedic doctor had told me long ago. She had asked me to decrease my Pitta dosha. Pitta in Ayurveda refers to a body type with a fast metabolism, wherein the gastrointestinal tract is hot and dry. I was initially not taking these concepts seriously, but as I started following her advice—taking two spoons of cow ghee (to lubricate and cool down the gastrointestinal tract, which is usually advised in the case of Pitta dosha) and roasted jeera (cumin) after meals to cool down hotness as prescribed—there was a considerable improvement in just two days. On the third day, the pain disappeared completely. I was quite surprised by the results. I could not believe the benefits of these indigenous methods. The moment I stopped taking ghee, I again started feeling pain in my neck. So I stuck to the regime, and have not faced any issues so far.

After this experience, I started studying Ayurveda and consulted other Ayurvedic doctors to know more about the Pitta anomaly. Those with a Pitta body type must avoid sour and salty eatables (as it increases Pitta). You need to find your cure based on your body type. Pitta body-type people are said to be prone to anxiety (which I am), while Kapha body-type people are said to be prone to irritation. So, do not take these concepts lightly and educate yourself about the classifications. You can consult a doctor or read up online and start taking precautions accordingly.

Pitta dosha-anomaly	Kapha dosha-anomaly	Vata dosha-anomaly[34]
The heat energy/dryness in the body is invisible. It manifests itself in your metabolism. People with this dosha are impatient, prone to conflict and always hungry (and likely to have mood swings because of it). They are also prone to acne and inflammation and sensitive to hot temperatures.	People with this dosha are described as robust, thick-boned and caring. They're known for keeping things together and being a support system for others. They have a slow metabolism and are prone to weight gain. They display sluggishness, tend to oversleep and are prone to breathing issues (i.e. asthma, allergies), heart diseases and depression. They need motivation.	Those with the Vata dosha are usually described as slim, energetic and creative. They're known for thinking outside the box but can become easily distracted. They are prone to forgetfulness, anxiety and mood swings, and are overwhelmed easily. They are highly sensitive to cold, have trouble sleeping and are prone to digestive issues and poor circulation.

[34]Ghosh, Debosmita, 'Ayurvedic Personality Types: All About Vata, Kapha and Pitta Dosha and Characteristics as Defined in Ayurveda', *Times Now*, 3 January 2023, https://www.timesnownews.com/spiritual/ayurvedic-personality-types-all-about-vata-kapha-and-pitta-dosha-and-characteristics-as-defined-in-ayurveda-article-96708259#. Accessed on 4 June 2023.

These are simple concepts but an imbalance may have a cumulative effect on your body. So, take help and start working on these small changes that can significantly improve the quality of your life.

Start consuming and avoiding eatables according to your body type.

Vata
Take these to calm and pacify Vata:
• Warm and cooked food • Hot beverages • Soft and moist food such as soups • Oily foods and ghee • Sweet food
Strictly avoid these to avoid aggravating Vata:
• Dry, crunchy food • Cold food • Vegan lifestyle

Pitta
Take these to calm and pacify Pitta:
• Juice • Coconuts and melons • Food with high water content (such as cucumber) • Drinks that are at room temperature or lukewarm • Two spoons of cow ghee before meals and roasted cumin
Strictly avoid these to avoid aggravating Pitta:
• Spicy food • Sour food • Acidic food, e.g. dishes/meals containing vinegar • Salty food

Kapha
Take these to calm and pacify Kapha:
• Warm cooked food • Dry food • Light food, low in fat and oil • Hot or warm beverages • Preferably vegetarian or vegan
Strictly avoid these to avoid aggravating Kapha:
• Heavy and large quantities of food, especially during the night • Cold food or cold beverages

Let's come to the next important issue in terms of diet. Our body, including the gastrointestinal tract, consists of billions of bacteria and microbiota that are either good or bad. These microorganisms are the drug-producing factories living in our bodies generating neurotransmitters. The right balance of good microorganisms is essential for good health. Whatever we eat is not only for us but also for the microorganisms living in us. We need to feed the good microorganisms too.

Is homemade food the answer? Well, let's see. Now, what is happening in the gut is similar to what's happening in a farm field. Consider a wheat or rice farm where monoculture is the standard practice. This means that there is not much scope to cultivate a variety of crops at the same time in a given area. Now, the condition in our gut is the same. How? Since the fibre content we consume, which is fed to our microbiota in the gut, is limited, the diversity in our gut has reduced, just like in the farm fields.[35] Almost everything is made from

---

[35]Cronin, Peter, Susan A. Joyce, Paul W. O'Toole, and Eibhlís M. O'Connor, 'Dietary Fibre Modulates the Gut Microbiota', *Nutrients*, Vol. 13, No. 5, 2021, 1655. https://doi.org/10.3390%2Fnu13051655.

wheat and rice! The Green Revolution has contributed to food security, but it has also led to changes in our gut that, in turn, have triggered a 'chronic illness revolution' in our modern society. Moreover, wheat and rice have a high glycaemic index, which means that they release more carbohydrates into the blood, putting the pancreas-producing insulin under pressure and increasing the risk of contracting diabetes. Our generation is being fed the worst kind of food—monotonous and high in carbohydrates (sugar). This is the fundamental anomaly triggering chronic illnesses in us and it persists even if we are eating the so-called 'safe' homemade food.

Are you eating the grains or are the grains eating you?

Dr Khadar Vali from Mysore, known as the 'Millet Man of India', and Dr A.S. Azad from Patiala have classified the grains into three categories: negative grains, neutral grains and positive grains.[36]

Negative grains (wheat and rice) gradually push you towards bad health in the long run. The impact of wheat and rice on our health differs from person to person and can take different forms. Neutral grains won't harm your health but they will not help you recover from bad health. Positive grains/millets have the capability to help you recover from chronic illnesses.

When I started taking positive grains, I could tell the difference in a matter of 15 days. Around August, I started taking millet, and by mid-September, there was considerable improvement in my health—my anxiety levels dropped and

---

[36]Prasad, Sanath, 'Unsung Heroes: Millet Man of India Dr Khadar Vali is Driving a Silent Revolution', *The Indian Express*, 11 February 2023, https://indianexpress. com/article/cities/bangalore/unsung-heroes-millet-man-of-india-dr-khadar-vali-is-driving-a-silent-revolution-8438370/. Accessed on 4 June 2023.

the problem of heart palpitations was also under control. Apart from the five grains, I kept eating other kinds of food as well. A combination of factors—eating a heavy diet, feeling lonely and some negative experiences—was triggering my SNS, causing anxiety, heart palpitations and fatigue. Millet intake helped me recover from these issues and today, I am completely off medicines. Yes, there have been times (even during the recovery period) when a mild gastrointestinal infection has triggered anxiety and heart palpitations, but with time, this has been brought under control.

Positive grains/ Millets	Neutral grains/Millets	Negative grains/ Millets[37]
Foxtail millet	Pearl millet (bajra)	Wheat
Barnyard millet	Finger millet (ragi or madua)	Paddy (rice)
Kodo millet	Proso millet (chena or pingu)	
Little millet	Great millet (mahan bajra)	
Browntop millet	Desi corn (makki)	

Indigenous names of millets					
English	Hindi	Marathi	Tamil	Kannada	Telugu
Barnyard Millet	Sanwa	–	Kuthiraivally	Oodhalu	Udhalu
Kodo Millet	Kodon	Kodro	Varagu	Arka	Arikelu
Little Millet	Kutki	Vari	Samai	Saame	Samulu
Foxtail Millet	Kakum	Rala	Tenai	Navane	Korra
Browntop Millet	Makra or Muradh	–	Palapul or Kula samai	Korale	Andu korralu

[37]Chauhan, Vikram, 'Millets Benefits - Positive, Negative and Neutral Millets', *Diet*, 23 January 2023, https://www.articlecube.com/millets-benefits-positive-negative-and-neutral-millets. Accessed on 5 June 2023.

INCORPORATE POSITIVE GRAINS IN YOUR DIET

When you're making a change in your food intake, remember to do it in a phased manner. So, for the first two days, you can try barnyard millet. You can make a chapati using a mixture of jowar and ragi (two-thirds jowar and one-third ragi). The next time you can make a porridge (after soaking it for 6–8 hours), and the third time you can experiment further or have porridge again. You can repeat these preparations for the other millet varieties (Kodo millet, little millet, foxtail millet and browntop millet), eating each of them for two days. Once you are at the end of the cycle, i.e. after two days of browntop millet, switch to barnyard millet and repeat the cycle.

Things to remember

Eat seasonal fruits	Balance your Vata/Pitta/Kapha anomaly	Eat millets

Start taking good prebiotic and probiotic capsules for 3-4 weeks; it will help you in recolonizing your gut with good bacteria.

The next step was to cut off milk from my diet. I used to take 2–3 cups of milk tea in the office; so, rather than not drinking tea at all, I switched to black tea. I didn't want to make any abrupt changes. After two or three days of drinking tea without milk, I noticed a spike in my energy. This turned out to be a good decision. (Milk, in some case studies, has been known to create neurological disorders.[38])

---

[38]Wu, Lei, and Dali Sun, 'Meta-Analysis of Milk Consumption and the Risk of Cognitive Disorders', *Nutrients*, Vol. 8, No. 12, 2016, 824. https://doi.org/10.3390%2Fnu8120824.

Abandoning milk gave me an energy boost. For calcium, eating fresh fruits and vegetables is better. Also, we can soak a small quantity of flax seeds or chia seeds in water for 5–6 hours in the morning, and then eat them in the evening. (Never eat them raw for they may create unnecessary heat or cause constipation.)

Over the years, I have been trying to find the root cause of anxiety, depression and OCD. I have finally concluded that my mental/emotional suffering was the effect but the cause was gut health. Whenever my gut was healthy, there was a significant drop in depression, anxiety and related issues. With each step, like balancing the body dosha and eating millet and fruits, my mental health was getting a booster dose. Just thinking about having a good gut will not help you. Whether it is triggering symptoms or not, we should still try the measures mentioned earlier and chalk out their path. The father of medicine, Hippocrates, and Ayurveda have pointed out that gut issues cause diseases, and from personal experience I can tell that this is indeed true.

> In my case I observed that eating wheat, or even the mixture of dry jowar and ragi or positive millet, was not enough to bring down my anxiety and stabilize my heart rate. Hydration is equally important. It's better to reduce flour chapatis to 2–3 per day and increase the intake of fruits and porridge. This will increase the water level in your body. It's always better to raise the water content in your body through fruits rather than drinking water directly.

While switching to other grains and abandoning wheat, we generally lose our sense of satisfaction from eating. We should be mentally prepared for this. However, after 1-2 months, we usually forget this so-called sense of satisfaction.

Also, when you're off wheat, you may face symptoms like headaches, which may make you think that abandoning wheat was perhaps not the right decision. However, these are withdrawal symptoms of high-carb diets such as wheat.

So, don't stop everything at one go; start experimenting with the food in a gradual and phased manner. This will help you in two ways: you will become aware of the issues affecting your body, and your body will get time to slowly tackle the withdrawal issues.

Let me share an example. Tanuj, assistant professor at a university in Jammu, was losing weight and couldn't wake up early in the morning. He used to wake up between 10.00 a.m. and 11.00 a.m. He wanted to improve his lifestyle and reset his sleep-wake cycle, but he couldn't. After being on medicines for some time, the doctor asked him to get tested for gluten intolerance. He subsequently tested positive for gluten sensitivity, so he stopped eating wheat and soon his sleep-wake cycle became normal and he felt energetic.

Although I had tested negative for gluten sensitivity, regulating my wheat intake has helped me recover. As mentioned earlier, I was advised by the doctor to stop taking paroxetine at some point. However, within six months, problems of anxiety and depression resurfaced. My sleep-wake cycle was disrupted. While on paroxetine, I was sleeping around 10.00 p.m. and waking up between 4.30 a.m. and 5.00 a.m. After I stopped taking the medication, I started waking up late, between 8.00 a.m. and 9.00 a.m. During this period, I tried a flour mixture consisting of jowar, jau, wheat husk, cumin and psyllium husk. Surprisingly, I started waking up around 6.00 a.m. thereafter. However, as you already know, I could not continue with this combination because it did not give me enough carbohydrates, which lowered my energy levels.

Lesson: If you feel heavy after waking up (sleep inertia) in the morning, it could be that your diet is too heavy (wheat, for example, is heavy and difficult to digest). As you age, you must understand that your digestive system has changed and you must consider switching to neutral and positive grains and include fruits. You will see that the heaviness will start dropping in a matter of 2–3 days.

Another example will be that of Ankur Jain, who lives in Ludhiana and had diplopia (double vision) and facial nerve palsy (a condition that causes sudden weakness in the muscles on one side of the face). He consulted several doctors, tried different medicines and lately was on steroids. However, he did not get much relief until he changed his diet, incorporating the five varieties of positive millet. He prefers them in the form of porridge. He has been off medication for three years now and his general health has also improved.

If you happen to know people who have recovered from horrible diseases, you may decide to ask what measures they took. Did they add millet to their diet as well? Why don't you ask around and find out for yourself?

Tip: Some drink hot water in the morning just after waking up. It's better to drink lukewarm water (±2 degrees of your body temperature). Too hot and too cold water may lead to more acid formation in the gastrointestinal tract.

MY DIET

- Two stuffed aloo paranthas made of a mixture of jowar and millet flour, and occasionally ragi. (The flour mixture can be made of any of the five positive grains mentioned earlier.)
- I drink black/green tea (no milk at all). I gave up drinking lime water regularly in the morning for the same reason— to avoid aggravating my pitta dosha).
- I carry a box of fruits (around 600–700 grams) to office; I prefer eating 3–4 seasonal fruits and salad. I don't eat them all together. I have some of them around two hours before lunch and then again around 2–3 hours after lunch.
- For lunch, I eat porridge made from any of the five positive grains.
- In the evening, I generally eat wheat-free biscuits or fruits like bananas. I also eat soaked chia seeds or flax seeds in the evening.
- For dinner, I sometimes eat rice; although it doesn't seem to harm me as such, I still try to stay away from it. (I intend to stop eating it soon.)

◆

Now that we have had plenty to eat and drink, let's move on to the movement aspect that's as important as eating right. In fact, something as simple as taking a walk after eating can work wonders for your health.[39]

---

[39]Cronkleton, Emily, 'Is Walking After Eating Good for You?', *Healthline*, 1 April 2020, https://www.healthline.com/health/walking-meditation. Accessed on 6 June 2023.

8

Physical Exercise as a Stress Buster

If you don't find time for today's fitness,
you are saving that time for tomorrow's sickness.

—Anonymous

We must realize that the body, including our brain, is not just our body. The body we have today is inherited from our parents, and this has been happening from the time our ancestors appeared on this planet. And you will be surprised to know how much your brain loves physical exercise, which also acts as a stress buster, thereby easing depression and anxiety symptoms.[40]

This complex system (our body) has evolved over millions of years. If we trace our ancestry, we were first climbers, then walkers, and gradually we became runners. But why we came down from the primary habitats, i.e. trees, and started walking on the ground is a mystery. We are the only ones who are bipedal and have a functional level of the brain higher than 250 species of primates. Lucy Lebanon Sofia (a primate whose fossil was discovered in Ethiopia), our ancestor from about 3.2 million years ago, walked on two legs and was barely

---

[40]'Depression and Anxiety: Exercise Eases Symptoms', *Mayo Clinic*, 27 September 2017, https://www.mayoclinic.org/diseases-conditions/depression/in-depth/depression-and-exercise/art-20046495. Accessed on 6 June 2023.

three and a half feet tall.[41] Fossils are proving that 6 million years ago, our ancestors were walking, but we needed more evolution to run; it took 3.8 million years for our bodies to do that.

Our body and brain constitute the biological system that has been designed by nature for hunting and gathering activities. We have spent a million years remaining social and hunting in groups as we didn't have speedy movement, poison to wade off animals, sharp teeth and wings to fly away from danger. The only thing we had was our brain, mysteriously designed to stay socially connected, create tools and share knowledge and experience through the ability to speak.

At a very later stage, we shifted to agriculture and decided on a more settled existence. The results were surprising. Fossil records show that our brains shrank by about 1500–1350 cc, i.e. roughly the size of a tennis ball.[42] Why? No one knows. The reason behind this may be the agricultural way of living, which was different from our primitive ancestors. We inculcated less walking and running, along with major changes in diet.

---

[41]"What Was "Lucy"? Fast Facts on an Early Human Ancestor', *National Geographic*, 20 September 2006, https://www.nationalgeographic.com/ history/article/lucy-facts-on-early-human-ancestor. Accessed on 5 June 2023.

[42]Ratner, Paul, 'Can Collective Intelligence be the Reason Why Human Brains are Shrinking?', *Interesting Engineering*, 23 November 2021, https:// interestingengineering.com/science/can-collective-intelligence-be-the- reason-why-human-brains-are-shrinking. Accessed on 12 May 2023.

Physically active lifestyle in the recent past

WHY DO WE NEED PHYSICAL EXERCISE?

*If there were a drug that could do for human health
everything that exercise can, it would likely be the
most valuable pharmaceutical ever developed.*

—Dr Mark Tarnopolsky

When we hear about mental ailments, anxiety, stress and depression, the concept of chemical imbalance strikes our mind and medicine seems to be the only solution. Being a social stigma, we hesitate to take medicine for mental illnesses. Exercise has, however, been underrated as the most potent antidepressant. British scientists conducted a study on cigarette cravings in smokers before and after exercise. They found that in smokers who craved a smoke before exercising, their orbitofrontal cortex showed higher activity in the scan. However, when the same group was made to exercise for 15 minutes, it showed less activity in these areas of the brain, thus exhibiting a considerable drop in craving.

In another test, Zoloft, a common antidepressant medicine, was given to one group of patients and another group was made to do physical exercise for a 16-week trial. The result of the group that was advised to do physical exercise (thrice a week) felt much better than the group of patients that was advised to take medicine. **(If you are on medicines, do not discontinue your prescribed medicines. The purpose is to apprise you about the relevance of physical movement and exercise.)**

In yet another interesting study, Jerry Morris, a doctor at Britain's Medical Research Council, conducted a study in 1940 about the linkage of coronary disease with a person who is physically active.[43] He studied the activity levels of bus drivers and conductors of the famous double-decker buses of London. The drivers were spending most of their time in the driver's seat and conductors on their legs, moving up and down during their shifts throughout their professional life. The study took two years and he tracked down 35,000 drivers and conductors; the results were astounding. Drivers were likely to have a double probability of cardiac arrests as compared to conductors, illustrating a strong link between being physically active and healthy.

In Japan, the importance of regular exercise has long been recognized. Rajio taisō (literally, 'radio exercises' or radio callisthenics), a music-based exercise, is played on the radio every day at 6.30 a.m. since 1928 to encourage citizens to be fit and healthy. It instructs the listeners to jump forwards and backwards, stretch their joints and roll their hips to the beat of a cheerful tune.

When neurotransmitters like dopamine, serotonin and norepinephrine are in deficit, people generally experience depression, anxiety, overthinking and OCD. Japanese researchers have found out that there was a considerable change in blood flow in the brain of a person who rode a bicycle for 15 minutes. A workout increased activity in various parts of the brain and led to an increase in the production of the antidepressant neurotransmitter—the happy hormone, serotonin.

Some American companies who wanted to develop the habit of exercising among their employees gave them a Fitbit

[43]Kuper, Simon, 'The Man Who Invented Exercise', *Financial Times*, 11 September 2009, https://www.ft.com/content/e6ff90ea-9da2-11de-9f4a-00144 feabdc0. Accessed on 12 May 2023.

activity tracker and found that the more the employees are physically active, the more they are incentivized to work. Various studies have found that people who sit more than eight hours a day without physical activity face an increased risk of dying early, much like people who smoke or are obese. Such people are doubly vulnerable to developing diabetes and cardiovascular complications.

YOUR BRAIN LOVES PHYSICAL EXERCISE

Serotonin stabilizes our mood, feeling of well-being and happiness.

Dopamine plays a role in feeling pleasure, motivation, focusing and learning.

Brain-derived neurotrophic factor (BDNF) is produced in the brain, which helps in repairing neurons and prevents neural degeneration.

Endorphins are produced in the pituitary gland and can act in both the central nervous system (CNS) and the peripheral nervous system (PNS) in response to pain and relieves stress.

Norepinephrine, also known as noradrenaline, plays an important role in your body's flight-or-fight response. As a medication, norepinephrine is used to increase and maintain blood pressure.

Blood flow increases the supply of oxygen and nutrients, and also removes waste, thus contributing to the rejuvenation of the brain.

Hippocampus is responsible for memory and learning and increases in size when you exercise regularly.

Running also stimulates the production of endorphins, a type of neurotransmitter that acts as our body's natural pain reliever,[44] just like Vicodin or morphine known for reducing

---

[44]Pugle, Michelle, 'What Are Endorphins?', *Verywell Health*, 26 July 2021,

pain and providing relief from stress and anxiety. **Regular exercise increases the resilient nature of not only physical but also emotional pain.** Endocannabinoids, which are naturally occurring chemicals in your brain, reduce pain sensitivity.

Some say that the brain-derived neurotrophic factor (BDNF) is the fertilizer that triggers a set of actions in the brain to rejuvenate brain cells.[45] But it takes time to show results. We usually have the habit of seeking instant results, but when we set the ball rolling in the positive direction, physical workouts increase the nerve growth factor, such as BDNF, and make our minds resistant to stress, anxiety and depression. Research has found that exercising rats who had voluntarily engaged in some kind of activity or running manifested the growth of neurons in the brain, especially in the hippocampus.[46]

> BDNF is a protein found in regions of the brain that control eating, drinking and body weight. It contributes to the management of these functions. It helps nerve cells survive and remain active in the brain at the connections between nerve cells. It regulates the process, which is important for learning and memory.

https://www.verywellhealth.com/endorphins-definition-5189854. Accessed on 5 June 2023.

[45]Renew & Protect Your Brain Cells | Brain Derived Neurotrophic Factor—Dr. Berg on Neurogenesis, YouTube, https://www.youtube.com/watch?v=XjQdUB-4QWs. Accessed on 5 June 2023.

[46]Nokia, Miriam S., Sanna Lensu, Juha P. Ahtiainen, Petra P. Johansson, Lauren G. Koch, Steven L. Britton and Heikki Kainulainen, 'Physical Exercise Increases Adult Hippocampal Neurogenesis in Male Rats Provided It is Aerobic and Sustained', *The Journal of Physiology*, Vol. 594, No. 7, 2016, 1855–1873. https://doi.org/10.1113%2FJP271552.

Apart from this, norepinephrine, a neurotransmitter, is also targeted by antidepressant medicines. Research shows that intense exercise like jogging helps increase the production of this neurotransmitter,[47] which levels up the quality of feeling and concentration in the mind.

> Neurotransmitters are chemical substances produced inside the nerve cells called neurons. They transmit signals from one neuron to the next target cell. When the brain perceives the occurrence of an event, brain cells, i.e. neurons, are activated, and neurotransmitters are released. These neurotransmitters are received by other cells through receptors. They are basically chemical messengers in the brain.

When we perform physical exercises, the muscles, joints, spinal cord and every part of the body, including the brain, interact with one another, so exercising or being physically active means stimulating the vital parts of your body including the brain. That means physical exercise is also a brain exercise.

This body we inherit is made for movement. Walking is one of the most fundamental activities and also the most effective antidepressant. Even a baby who has not learned to talk starts walking because the genes are programmed to give the baby the innate strength to walk on two legs. Walking is instinctual; thus, whenever and wherever you find free time, just stand up and move around.

---

[47]Basso, Julia C., and Wendy A. Suzuki, 'The Effects of Acute Exercise on Mood, Cognition, Neurophysiology, and Neurochemical Pathways: A Review', *Brain Plasticity*, Vol. 2, No. 2, 2017, 127–152. https://doi.org/10.3233%2FBPL-160040.

Why do we have a brain?

Neuroscientist Daniel Wolpert says that we have a brain to primarily produce adaptable and complex movements of the body.[48] For example, the koala bear, which is a very slow animal, has a brain that has shrunk and has therefore reduced its physical movements and increased its dependence on a narrower range of food.

One day, a colleague of mine found that when he would stand up and start walking, his feet felt as if there were cushions underneath. Well-known neurologists that he consulted could not diagnose the reason for this and prescribed medicines with little respite. After a while, he started going to a gym and did stationery cycling and soon felt a sense of temporary relief. As he increased his workout time, he felt better for longer and longer periods. As time passed, the period of relief kept increasing. This tells us that the body has its mysterious ways of healing, provided we enable it to do so in a natural manner. So always stay physically active.

How to Start Exercising?

Think! If you spend 60 minutes exercising every day, you can calculate that you have spent 60 minutes × 30 days × 6 months = 10,800 minutes or 180 hours on health in the past six months. This will give your mind a boost both physically and mentally and help you keep working on your fitness level.

---

[48]The Real Reason for Brains - Daniel Wolpert, *YouTube*, https://www.youtube.com/watch?v=_DdU4ehCzUM. Accessed on 12 May 2023.

Walk half an hour every day in the morning with 5-10 minutes of running. Thereafter, you should exercise for some time. You can do simple exercises like the ones you did in school during physical training sessions. Do the normal back stretches and leg exercises. No special exercise is required, just move and let your heartbeat rise.

Doing more than this is your prerogative. Don't keep moving around in a small loop in your house—gradually increase your area of movement. Make it more interesting by adding other places to walk. As you start developing your love for morning walks, get a bicycle and explore the areas around your place. Before going for a morning walk, eat something, e.g. 2-3 dates or a banana, which can give you some energy. Note that waking up late disturbs your circadian rhythm and not eating on time can damage your brain as it cannot store food for itself, and thus, when it runs out of supply of energy, its health gets affected.

Further, always choose a home or office space where you get direct sunlight. The closer we are to natural elements, the happier our minds will be. This is just the way our bodies are designed. Respect the body clock and biology that have evolved through millions of years and they will respect you too.

If running on a treadmill, try and place it near a large window that will elevate your mood. Research shows that patients in hospitals who were near a window and who could track day and night recovered faster than those who were put in rooms without a window.

We can have issues such as constant anxiety, depression and mood swings but if we maintain a good mood while exercising, walking, running and stretching, it will provide us greater benefits than thinking negatively while working out or even walking. If we start manipulating our exercise schedule, we start compromising with the duration. Just like eating is necessary for the body, a workout is also a fundamental requirement of the body, and compromising it for office work or other activities is absolutely non-negotiable. If you start working out, your work performance and other activities will considerably change for the better. Unfortunately, we are not taught scientifically about the relevance of workouts. A regular workout stimulates your appetite and reduces your craving for junk food and your taste for healthy food gets enhanced.

Our sole purpose is to increase the physical activity of the body. When you don't feel like exercising, it means that negative circuits are taking control of your brain. Depressive feelings make you isolated and tend to keep you away from exercising and make it hard to concentrate.

Listen to happy songs rather than depressive music. Those who have a preference for bhakti music will find that it adds to their sense of well-being. Music involves most of the limbic system (part of the brain involved in our behavioural and emotional responses), the hippocampus, nucleus accumbens and pre-genual anterior cingulate cortex.[49]

[49]Koelsch, Stefan, 'Brain Correlates of Music-Evoked Emotions', *Nature Reviews Neuroscience*, Vol. 15, 2014, 170–180. https://doi.org/10.1038/nrn3666.

Free antidepressant drug

The brain requires around 20 per cent of the oxygen that enters through your bloodstream.[50] Energy consumption by the brain is more than any other organ, so less oxygen intake and improper breathing make it prone to damage due to oxygen insufficiency. Sit down in a relaxed position and inhale slowly and deeply, drawing maximum air into your lungs (note that when you inhale, your belly should expand). Stay in that position as per your total lung capacity. Then, exhale slowly. This exercise is known to relax the mind instantly. It stimulates the PNS in which pressure receptors, when stimulated by lung inflation, trigger the system that brings down the stress response of the body, thereby relaxing you.[51]

Find out interest groups (WhatsApp, Telegram and Instagram) that post content on relevant issues like health. Watch and make videos about your hobbies, like photography, history and drama; get involved in sports like cycling, running, jogging, shooting, football, volleyball, basketball, cricket, hockey, badminton, table tennis and athletics. Pick any sport you have played before or are familiar with.

---

[50]Michaud, Mark, 'Study Reveals Brain's Finely Tuned System of Energy Supply', *University of Rochester Medical Center*, 7 August 2016, https://www.urmc.rochester.edu/news/story/study-reveals-brains-finely-tuned-system-of-energy-supply. Accessed on 5 June 2023.
[51]Janzen, Anne, 'The Effects of Deep Breathing on the Brain: Why You Need It', *Somnox*, 5 August 2022, https://somnox.com/blog/the-effects-of-deep-breathing-on-the-brain-why-you-need-it/. Accessed on 5 June 2023.

Tip: Do not reduce your antidepressant medicine without the advice of a medical professional. However, when you do reduce the medicine (under a doctor's guidance), increase your exercise by 1.5 times; it will help you in tackling withdrawal symptoms.

Point to ponder!

This is an age of lifestyle diseases; chronic diseases are turning out to be a major cause of suffering and mortality. Although life spans are also increasing, but is the quality of life increasing?

We remain on autopilot mode most of the time if we have healthy habits. That means we don't need to push ourselves because we are automatically driven to sleep early, wake up early and go for morning walks. But, when our habits are anti-body and anti-brain, the autopilot mode will keep us awake till 1.00 a.m. or 2.00 a.m., throwing off our entire routine—we won't go for morning walks or have time for exercise; instead, we will spend time in front of screens.

Lack of Interest in Physical Activity

There's something wrong if your body doesn't crave physical exercise because your body may be craving junk food, alcohol or other harmful consumables. You will have to change the craving of the body from such habits to a craving for physical exercise, which is the most potent drug whenever your body feels low. That is what biological evolution has ordained for us.

I never had any sort of inclination towards physical exercise. However, I went to the gym, which was only 20–50 metres away from where I lived. Nothing happened in the first month. But when I didn't go for a week, my body and mind started craving movement and physical exercise. Even today, if I have a headache, I go for an hour-long walk, rather than taking a pill, and it helps tremendously. I do the same when I have back pain, blurred vision or when I have had too much screen time. Most of my friends also say that they engage in light exercises like push-ups when they feel stressed. That's the way they deal with it.

WHAT'S THE IDEAL WAY TO BUST STRESS?

Why is the fight-or-flight response triggered? The hippocampus stores negative experiences as memories and analyses threats in terms of past experiences. So, when the hippocampus perceives a threat, it sends out an alert to other parts of the brain, and the amygdala (emotional brain) is activated, thereby releasing cortisol and catecholamines and the logical decision-maker (prefrontal cortex) is unable to make the right judgement.[52] Then, the SNS comes into play, the heart rate increases, blood pressure rises, there is rapid breathing, the mind becomes more focussed to react, and thus, the body becomes ready for the fight-or-flight response.

When the heart rate and blood pressure increase, the blood supply to the intestines is reduced as blood is directed to the legs and muscles so that physical activity can be performed in order to escape any sort of danger.

---

[52]'Posttraumatic Stress Disorder and Neurochemical Processes', *European Medical*, 4 February 2023, https://www.europeanmedical.info/posttraumatic-stress/posttraumatic-stress-disorder-and-neurochemical-processes.html. Accessed on 6 June 2023.

When the uncomfortable or threatening situation goes away, we still retain the high cortisol levels in the body as our body was expecting us to run, but we didn't. That would actually be followed by a reduction in cortisol levels.

Now, let's see what high cortisol levels mean. Too much release of cortisol may cause other conditions and symptoms, including high blood pressure, type 2 diabetes, impaired brain function, fatigue and infections.

Our ancestors would have fought or run (flight), but what do we do now to switch off the fight-or-flight response and lower the cortisol levels?

The answer is physical exercise, the simplest one being walking. Just imitate our ancestors.

> **Take help:** If you have an issue regarding mobility and cannot perform an exercise, consult your doctor about what kind of exercises you need to undertake. Staring at the sea to cross it will not get you anywhere; similarly, just understanding the benefits of a workout will not provide you with good mental health until you actually engage in it.

> **Think:** By walking and running for millions of years, the human body evolved, whereas nowadays, most of us hardly walk or run, leading to a sedentary lifestyle.
>
> Children go through so much stress these days. Do you think that children millions of years ago were as competitive and stressed because of information, studies and peer pressure, as today's children are? Therefore, how much more prone are today's children to chronic ailments, both physically and mentally?

Just imagine!

Our primitive ancestors were moving 10-20 kilometres on an average daily;[53] climbing, sprinting and stretching their muscles; moving in groups and dealing with various uncertainties of life; facing intense sunlight and sleeping during nightfall.

We inherited the body of that ancestor and till today, nothing much has changed. With the body of hunters and

---

[53]King, Anthony, 'Evolved to Run—But Not to Exercise', *The Irish Times*, 3 December 2020, https://www.irishtimes.com/news/science/evolved-to-run-but-not-to-exercise-1.4412604. Accessed on 6 June 2023.

gatherers, we are living a sedentary lifestyle in modern civilization.

So, as far as possible, going back to that original lifestyle for which this body is made will resolve most of our problems.

Along with battling our brain for dominance, feeding both our bodies and brains the things that are best for them and exercising to keep ourselves sane as well as fit, another important factor that we are yet to explore is resting or taking a pause or sleeping, by whatever name you want to mention it.

9

Secrets Nobody Tells You About Sleep

The shorter your sleep, the shorter your life span.

—Matthew Walker

You might have studied the GIGO, i.e. 'garbage in, garbage out' principle in your computer classes. If you put garbage into your computer, garbage will come out. It's the same case with us. Let's see how.

Have you ever wondered why our elders told us to pray to god before going to sleep? Why did our grandmothers and grandfathers recite prayers and why did moms tell beautiful fairy tales to their children and not those of devils? Like the law of gravity states that all bodies having a mass will fall towards Earth, there is a simple rule for our sleep as well. Allow me to reveal the secrets that nobody tells you about sleep.

Do you go to sleep every day with gratitude and good feelings?

Any thoughts/emotions/feelings you feed your mind before going to sleep will be worked upon by your brain while sleeping because, though our conscious mind might sleep, our subconscious mind keeps on working on the last thoughts of the day. These feelings can be those of anger, frustration, depression, deprivation, jealousy or love, affection, devotion, gratitude and service. The subconscious mind does not differentiate between good and bad feelings—as you sow, so shall you reap, which means you will get returns but in a more amplified way.

Now, the utility of this knowledge, or more appropriately, wisdom, is that you should become conscious of your feelings when you go to sleep so that you can programme your mind. For example, if you recite prayers, you develop devotional feelings, become relaxed and then go to sleep. In that case, you can feel the difference minutely the next day. Repeat it for 3-4 days and you will start seeing the difference. Conversely, if you go to sleep with anger and frustration after fighting with your spouse every night, the quality of your life will be vastly different. Habits will pay you dividends in the short as well as the long run. Students can use this method to feel good about their studies. So, if you want to change your way of life, then this should be one of the first steps—to change your feelings/ emotional patterns that will pave the way for the next level of improvement. And for those who have anxiety, depression or are experiencing a hard time, this will be a boon for them.

So, let me ask you again, do you go to sleep every day with gratitude and good feelings?

HOW DOES THE ABOVE WORK?

Our brain possesses the capability to adapt to our environment and belief system throughout life. New neural patterns are formed that relax and make the mind healthier. Not getting good quality sleep and its deprivation leads to cognitive impairments, especially in memory and learning, and various other unforeseen issues connected with the brain.

THE BODY SAYS 'TIT FOR TAT'

In 1971, Allan Rechtschaffen, a world-renowned sleep research pioneer at the University of Chicago, stated, 'If sleep does not serve an absolutely vital function, then it is the biggest mistake the evolutionary process has ever made.'[54] Sleep quality is vital to all living species, as much as eating and drinking. An average healthy person needs 8 hours of quality sleep daily, which leaves 16 hours for other activities. It's such a vital part of our existence that we spend 33 per cent of our life span sleeping.

Sleeping more than 8-9 hours can also be a symptom of bad mental health as your brain requires more time to recharge itself and the body, and this may be because of some form of anxiety, depression, imbalanced nutrition or a sedentary lifestyle.

The issue is not about waking up early, but about going to sleep early. Then everything will fall into place. Early to bed (with good feelings) and early to rise (with good feelings) makes a man healthy, wealthy and wise.

 Do you get 8 hours of quality sleep every day?

As I mentioned earlier, **our body and brain are not just our own**; rather, we inherited them from our ancestors whose bodies and brains evolved through millions of years. We inherit the same mechanism of actions and reactions and processes that they had. Therefore, the hypothalamus in our

[54]Wood, Matt, 'Renowned Researcher Helped Illuminate the Detrimental Effects of Sleep Deprivation', *UChicago News*, 13 December 2021, https://news. uchicago.edu/story/allan-rechtschaffen-sleep-research-pioneer-1927-2021. Accessed on 17 July 2023.

brain is known to regulate our sleep cycles. The pineal gland functions in response to light. When there is darkness, it secretes melatonin and when it reaches threshold level and is received by the hypothalamus, we fall asleep. During daylight hours, the pineal gland reduces melatonin production.[55] This is the instinct that our body has inherited from our ancestors. If we need to be healthy, we need to follow the rules of the body set by nature. Otherwise, it will be tit for tat—not taking care of the body will make you pay in the form of diseases, unrest, anxiety and so on.

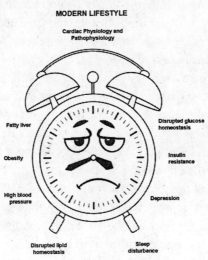

Disturbed Circadian Rhythm

For those suffering from insomnia, melatonin is given externally. Certain tissues in the body generate melatonin but the major source is the pineal gland located in the brain where

---

[55]'Melatonin', *Cleveland Clinic*, 5 July 2022, https://my.clevelandclinic.org/health/articles/23411-melatonin. Accessed on 7 June 2023.

it is produced from the amino acid tryptophan at night time.[56] It is sensed by reduced light entering the eyes. This biological cycle that is synchronized by daylight and darkness at night is called the sleep–wake cycle or the circadian rhythm.

IMPORTANCE OF THE SLEEP-WAKE CYCLE

Reduction in sleep is directly linked with the quality of work, creativity, flexibility and concentration levels. The continuous repetition of such a pattern also has a direct impact on the decline of our cognitive abilities, which gradually leads to a deterioration of the mind's health. The prefrontal cortex, the crucial part of the brain that makes us different from animals and is responsible for decision-making, controlling attention and self-expression slows down activity while sleeping. This means that the alertness of the mind is greatly affected. When staying up late becomes a habit, the activity of the prefrontal cortex is affected (i.e. the neural firing gets slower) and the mind becomes less creative and starts losing attention in the long term.[57] But by taking proper sleep at the right time, the functioning of the mind greatly improves.

Disturbed, low quality and insufficient sleep affect the working memory in the prefrontal cortex (which also contributes to setting and achieving goals, as we discussed above), and the amygdala (part of the brain involved with different emotional responses) starts showing more activity

---

[56]Zhao, Dake, Yang Yu, Yong Shen, Qin Liu, Zhiwei Zhao, Ramaswamy Sharma, and Russel J. Reiter, 'Melatonin Synthesis and Function: Evolutionary History in Animals and Plants', *Frontiers in Endocrinology*, Vol. 10, 2019, 249. https://doi.org/10.3389/fendo.2019.00249.

[57]Friedman, Naomi P., and Trevor W. Robbins, 'The Role of Prefrontal Cortex in Cognitive Control and Executive Function', *Neuropsychopharmacology*, Vol. 47, 2022, 72–89. https://doi.org/10.1038/s41386-021-01132-0.

than usual. This means you will start overreacting and become moody. Just imagine how a situation can change when you are not getting enough regular sleep.

While sleeping, the subconscious mind works in the background to consolidate memory. It keeps on solving jigsaw puzzles, arranging and rearranging memories, and throwing away unnecessary information while preserving relevant parts, such as what you see in dreams and your secrets—working of the mind is like rearranging scattered books in a library. Brain scans during sleep have shown the electrical impulses of the hippocampus, hypothalamus, cortex and brain stem being active with an ongoing process of shifting short-term memory to long-term memory.[58] It's as if the brain is making notes for a future exam—discarding information that it holds irrelevant.

> August Kekulé was a German organic chemist who discovered the structure of benzene in one of his daydreams. Larry Page once dreamed that he could download the entire web onto some computers lying around, which later on took the shape of Google.[59] Similarly, Elias Howe discovered the sewing machine and Dr James Watson discovered the double helix spiral structure of our DNA in a dream. We probably won't win a prize or make a breakthrough discovery or invention because of our dreams, but good sleep is still crucial if you are to use your potential to its optimal level.

[58] Fields, R. Douglas, 'Using Electricity, Researchers Find Surprising Memory Results', *Psychology Today*, 23 August 2022, https://www.psychologytoday.com/us/blog/the-new-brain/202208/using-electricity-researchers-find-surprising-memory-results. Accessed on 7 June 2023.

[59] Gillett, Rachel, 'Larry Page Created Google in His Sleep—Here's Why "Sleeping On It" Can Be Legitimately Productive', *Business Insider*, 5 May 2016, https://finance.yahoo.com/news/productive-while-youre-sleeping-125100995.html. Accessed on 7 June 2023.

The sleep–wake cycle affects the hunger hormone ghrelin, which is produced by the stomach when it is empty. The hormone travels through the blood, signalling to the mind a craving for food. It plays a key role in managing calorie intake and fat levels. If you are overweight, correcting the sleep–wake cycle will have a positive result on your hunger hormone production.

Due to abnormal patterns of sleep, the production of  other helpful hormones, such as leptin (that helps our body in maintaining our weight) and melatonin (that helps us in falling asleep quickly), which have anti-ageing and anti-cancer properties, is reduced in the brain.

Sleep deprivation increases cortisol levels in our body, which helps manage stress. The increase in this hormone burns up our body muscles and can put us in a constant aggressive/alert mode.

Sleep deprivation also increases the risk of neurodegenerative diseases. The rules set by evolution for our brain and body can trigger our systems into vicious loops of diseases, which may become difficult to manage.

The glymphatic system, which is a network of vessels that clears the waste from the central nervous system, works mostly during sleep. Brain cells shrink to allow cerebrospinal fluid to get into the brain and flush out the waste. Disturbed and irregular timings of sleep interfere with this system, which can have direct implications on the neurological health of our bodies.

Adenosine is produced by the burning of the chemical compound known as adenosine triphosphate in the neurons, and when this adenosine reaches a certain level, then the brain sends a signal to sleep.[60] However, if caffeine attaches itself to adenosine, thereby tricking the body that it is not the time to sleep, it interferes with the natural process. This is why drinking coffee, even 6–7 hours before sleep, is discouraged.

The production of the beta-amyloid protein, which comes in several different molecular forms—one of them the toxic beta-amyloid 42 related to Alzheimer's disease—increases when we do not get enough sleep. In patients with Alzheimer's, microglia (a type of glial cell), which usually engulfs and destroys waste and toxins in a healthy brain, fails to clear away waste, debris and protein collections including beta-amyloid plaques.[61]

Furthermore, as our body and brain developed through the process of evolution, we spent a lot of time under the sun, but currently, we are a sunlight-deprived generation, not as exposed to daylight as our forefathers were, who lived as hunter-gatherers or agriculturists.

Exposure to sunlight increases serotonin (the key hormone that stabilizes our mood, feelings of well-being and happiness). It is a second possible approach to increasing serotonin without drugs. Daylight is a treatment for seasonal depression but it is also helpful for non-seasonal depression. It has been seen through post-mortem examinations that serotonin levels are higher in those who died in summer than in those who died in winter. (These examinations were performed in sunlight-deficit regions of Europe.)

---

[60]Summer, Jay, and Dr Nilong Vyas, 'Adenosine and Sleep', *Sleep Foundation*, 10 June 2022, https://www.sleepfoundation.org/how-sleep-works/adenosine-and-sleep. Accessed on 7 June 2023.

[61]'What Happens to the Brain in Alzheimer's Disease?', *National Institute on Aging*, 16 May 2017, https://www.nia.nih.gov/health/what-happens-brain-alzheimers-disease. Accessed on 7 June 2023.

On the contrary, by forcing our bodies to stay awake during the night while using gadgets, the internet or watching TV, we have made our bodies habituated to staying up late. This is mostly seen in the younger generation because of the round-the-clock availability of social media on hand-held gadgets (we will discuss this particularly in a later section). This generation has started suffering from chronic diseases due to lifestyle problems, and the sleep–wake cycle is one of the crucial causes for such issues, including depression.

The optimal sleep cycle time is from 8.00-10.00 p.m. to 4.00-6.00 a.m., which is when the brain is most productive to rejuvenate itself. Not adhering to this sleep cycle causes the body to go against natural laws and does not let the brain recharge itself for its normal functioning.

HOW TO IMPROVE YOUR LIFESTYLE?

Before going to sleep, pay attention to your feelings if you wish to bring peace to your mind and body.

If you do not believe in praying, you should nevertheless evoke a feeling of gratitude before sleeping—gratitude to everyone you met today, to nature for whatever good you have in life; even see the negative things that happened to you through a positive perspective. Or, you can watch something amusing on TV or read an interesting book instead of watching a horror movie and see to it that your children do not play violent video games.

If you fight with your spouse and go to sleep without resolving feelings of anger or resentment, these will work upon your subconscious mind all night. **Resolving issues before going to sleep is essential.**

Tip: Walking after dinner is good as it helps induce sleep when you lie down. Ensure that it is dark. Do not use a red light in the room and don't sleep in a noisy room.

Myth: Some say that they are night owls and can stay up late just as they did in college. This is just a myth as we have been biologically designed to work in the daytime. It weakens the general immune system and affects mental health horribly. The most affected are the young generation who, due to social media on hand-held gadgets and round-the-clock television, harm their healthy sleep–wake cycle.

Nicotine and caffeine sleep suppressors should not be taken at least 4-6 hours before going to bed as they disturb the quality of your sleep.

When sleep gets disturbed, it affects the slow-wave sleep phase, which is crucial for the brain, because it balances hormone levels and repairs tissues, among other things.[62]

Sleep deprivation can cause depression, or conversely, depression can cause sleep disorders; both are interlinked. In a majority of cases, depressive disorders because of lack of sleep can be easily identified.

Depression may lead to insomnia or excessive sleeping or depression may lead to insomnia aggravating the depression itself. It is a vicious loop.

---

[62]Newsom, Rob, and Dr Abhinav Singh, 'Slow-Wave Sleep', *Sleep Foundation*, 15 May 2023, https://www.sleepfoundation.org/stages-of-sleep/slow-wave-sleep. Accessed on 7 June 2023.

WAKE UP SID!

Sleeping late at night has become the new lifestyle. It harms the brain and is a creator of lifestyle troubles. But today, if you say you sleep at 9.00 p.m. to your friends, they may laugh at you. If you wake up late in the morning and are unable to change the habit, it becomes a problem because, again, you sleep late at night. **Try to fix this pattern of sleeping late.** When you sleep early, you will wake up early too. You can plan your day and everything will fall into place. You may need to renew your passport or driving license or pay electricity bills online, or you may want to go for a morning walk or devote some time to exercise or eat some protein-rich diet. For all other activities, including office work, household chores and hobbies, you will get ample time in the morning. This way you get the time to do some miscellaneous or other important work in the morning, and then, you start your day with satisfaction. That's the best way to remain satisfied and content all day and you feel less bored while performing your office job.

Waking up early reduces anxiety. For many, it's difficult to move out of bed in the morning. 'If you don't have the energy to climb mountains when you wake up in the morning, then it is a strong indication that your health is out of sync,' says my mentor Amar Singh Chandel.

If you wake up late, say, at 8.30 a.m. or 9.00 a.m., and you have to reach the office by 10.00 a.m., then you have to brush your teeth, have a shower, iron your clothes, skip the morning walk (an early morning walk regulates your biological clock every day) and exercise, skip answering nature's call, skip having breakfast and then start running towards office. As you perform all these activities hurriedly, you start developing small anxieties that always remain at the back of your mind.

As your day starts late, you stay behind your schedule. The point to note is that if you are practising this kind of haste and anxiety every day, you start internalizing it. Do you want this kind of life to continue?

How to start rising early?

1. Do pranayama for at least 10-20 minutes twice daily (I call it an anti-depressant pill, you try it and see the difference).
2. Have dinner around 8.00 p.m. and do not eat anything after that.
3. Change your diet from heavy grains like wheat to millet (which has already been discussed in Chapter 7).

Morning walk: Nothing can be a substitute for regular walks. Evidence from studying fossils proves that 6 million years ago, even our ancestors were walking. It's the most fundamental activity. As mentioned earlier, even before talking, a child tries to walk on two legs. There are numerous known and unknown advantages of the morning walk.

- Morning walks correct your body clock.
- They help you regulate and clean the bowel system; a happy tummy leads to a happy brain. We have already read about this in Chapter 6.
- Walking for one hour leads to serotonin production, the happy hormone, in the body.

SCROLLING THROUGH THE BLUES

On average, the younger generation spends around 3-6 hours online per day, which includes social media networks. Many of us check our social media accounts as we wake up, in our free time during the day, before going to sleep, and even in the middle of the night. Such addiction is largely due to dopamine, which is also released during gambling, drug addiction or when you smoke. The uncontrolled urge that takes over some of us is transforming us into digital zombies. This 'attention economy' is based on tapping our responses. Our personal preferences are tracked and the data collected is thereafter used to market products, grabbing our attention. Social media uses the user. The user becomes the commodity. The users are turned into addicts to make money. The preferences, habits, choices and user search history are used for making money so that advertisements for selling products can be shown to the user according to their needs and preferences.

This psychological addiction to social media affects the regions of attention, emotional processing and decision-making in the brain, similar to when we are addicted to some drug; obviously, the degree varies. Thus, the advent of social media has been responsible for a major shift in our cognitive skills, which further affects the quality of our life.

Technology binds us but somehow, it also makes us more isolated than ever before. We are losing person-to-person and social contact. Technology has also taken us away from social groups around us and we are paying the price for it. The process is so slow that we are unable to recognize its subtle impact on our body and mind.

When physical interaction or face-to-face contact is established, a larger part of the brain gets activated, whereas, during an interaction through social media, you are not involved in non-verbal communication, which is necessary for face-to-face interaction. When you are communicating digitally, you can't read the non-verbal cues of the other person. You are also aware of the cyber audience, which is obviously different from a physical audience.

The more we use social media, the more diminished our attention span, as surfing and usage of digital devices are anti-attention. On the contrary, an activity like meditation increases our attention span. Attention is required for day-to-day activities; it is linked to our ability to remember and communicate, which, when affected, may lead to serious repercussions in the long run. Smartphones have become smarter and the user has become less smart, whether it is for remembering lists, searching for places in the vicinity and so on. Social media is full of so much information that we develop the art of ignoring what is necessary; thus, our mind gets used to ignoring rather than learning things. For example, during a trip or an outdoor visit, we can see that our minds are more involved in taking selfies and photographs. We are gradually forgetting to live in the present. We remember how we took photographs rather than the actual place and what we did there.

Meditation, pranayama, reading books, exercise, etc. tend to have the opposite effect, prolonging our attention span. It is always advised to do one thing at a time, like avoiding using the phone during mealtimes as it messes with your attention span and also reduces the brain's ability to learn and memorize.

Opportunities that were once exclusive to celebrities, such as having a large following of people who constantly like and track your daily activities, having your pictures taken and getting public approval and appreciation, are now available to the common man too. Such actions provide immediate rewards without any physical or mental effort. Hence, the mind develops a craving for being liked and appreciated. We crave more of it as it is easily available. This drug of social media that is easily available and cheap is much more difficult to detoxify from. The reward centre produces more dopamine and craves more. Whenever there is some cause for anxiety, we move to social media and are stimulated and relaxed. But after some time, our anxiety is triggered again and the vicious loop continues.

> **Phantom vibration syndrome:** Here, the person carrying a device/mobile phone feels like they are getting a call or a message, for they say that they sense the vibration in their pocket or a bag where the phone is kept. This makes them check their phone but there is no call or message. This is how our nervous system reacts sometimes. However, this is not a serious issue but definitely worth exploring as a study of perceptions.[63]

When a person is not happy (which is usually the case among today's generation where many don't even know themselves but continue to be in a sad state for longer periods of time, which tends to become the new normal for them) or stressed and anxious, their minds can easily escape to social media forums that stimulate them in an easy and cheap way. Thus, the person becomes overly dependent on such routes of escape rather than looking for a real solution to their problems. Such people move between reality and the social media world like a shuttle, and this also leads to the obvious problem of procrastination. The younger generation will relate to you when there is some important work to be done and there

---

[63]'What is Phantom Vibration Syndrome?', *Ivan Allen College of Liberal Arts*, https://iac.gatech.edu/research/features/what-is-phantom-vibration-syndrome. Accessed on 7 June 2023.

is time to do that, but they keep delaying corrective action. Creating an account on social media is an identity project. It gives a person a sense of what kind of person they want to become. Once they have figured this out, they project this persona through their social media content. The image that we create for others on social media matches our expectations. It is a reflection of what a person aspires to become and thus begins the endless pursuit of fitting into the role.

Those who subconsciously feel some sort of identity crisis also get the opportunity to cling to some identity and become loud and unpleasant on social media when launching their campaign. It is all to get attention, which may be through unhealthy comments or posts. Many even go to the extent of offending others, hurling abuses at those who have different ethnic, religious or class identities. Some users are professional at making their fake accounts look real and target other vulnerable users by befriending them for money and committing other frauds.

Then there are the anonymous users, who feel more comfortable hiding their identity. They become more open, loud and unpleasant, and can make irresponsible remarks such as trolling. Another category in this virtual world is of those anonymous users who are mute spectators, observing people around them or stalking and tracking their targets or victims.

Also, when we watch uploaded pictures, videos and statuses of others who project themselves to be happier than others (mostly such images are photoshopped to portray fake happiness), we start comparing our reality with the fake reality of others. Always remember that comparison is the thief of joy.

When we get a good comment or a 'like' on our updated status, the reward centre is stimulated and dopamine is produced. The problem turns severe when a notification or a casual checking of the status, or the mere anticipation of a response, triggers the release of dopamine.

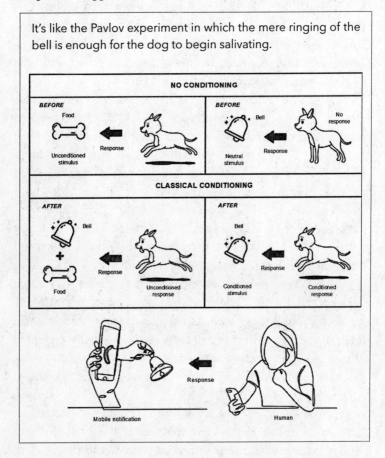

It's like the Pavlov experiment in which the mere ringing of the bell is enough for the dog to begin salivating.

NO CONDITIONING

BEFORE
Food
Unconditioned stimulus
Response

BEFORE
Bell
Neutral stimulus
Response
No response

CLASSICAL CONDITIONING

AFTER
Bell
+
Food
Response
Unconditioned response

AFTER
Bell
Response
Conditioned stimulus
Conditioned response

Mobile notification
Response
Human

So, what can we do? Dopamine detoxification or dopamine fasting, wherein we intentionally avoid phone/social media on alternative days, or once or twice a week to break the loop, is a way of tackling the issue. Today, there are even some paid applications that will lock your phone for a certain period of time as per your requirement so that you can concentrate on work.

The topic is new and still being researched. When a person clicks pictures and more than 50 per cent of them are selfies, then this is alarming. Clicking more than six selfies a day can be termed as 'selfitis' wherein the purpose of clicking pictures is to upload them on social media sites.[64] Taking three selfies a day but not necessarily posting them can be termed as 'borderline selfitis'. Posting selfies three times a day can be termed as 'acute selfitis'. The urge is due to the underlying feeling of loneliness or to boost confidence, or a manifestation of an attention-seeking attitude or simply for a feel-good factor. Rather than connecting with the family, we turn to social media. The relationships could be stronger in the family, but to gain self-importance for whatever reasons, some users turn to social media in an obsessive way.

Watching television, especially negative content, should be strictly avoided when you are depressed/anxious. News or content that activates the amygdala (the region of the brain primarily linked with emotional processes), triggering feelings of sex, jealousy, etc. is not good for you. You should instead shift your focus to hobbies or other activities, like travelling and so on. If you are watching negative content on television or social media, you are putting your mental health, which is already deteriorating, in the hands of the 'idiot box' or the 'idiot media', which is just using you to spike its profits.

---

[64]Hagen-Miller, Linda, 'Do You Know Somebody Who Suffers from "Selfitis"?', *Healthline*, 4 April 2018, https://www.healthline.com/health-news/do-you-know-somebody-who-suffers-from-selfitis. Accessed on 7 June 2023.

Therefore, switch off social media and switch on life. Now that you know all the secrets nobody tells you about sleep, sleep on time, dream big and live a fulfilling life. Am I forgetting something else? Ah, here goes...

10

The Avalanche Principle

Even the largest avalanche is triggered by small things.

—Vernor Vinge

Knowledge is power. The more we know ourselves, the better we can live. From the day we are born to when we die, we have our constant companion—our mind—which stays with us and makes us view our experiences through its lens; the mind is the interpreter of perceptions, the meaning maker. And there are certain principles or rules that determine how the mind works. Adhering to these will make you happy and content and you will enjoy a vibrant life. Working against these principles, whether knowingly or unknowingly, will cost you dearly. Here, we will talk about such a principle, giving you an insight into the mind's secret way of working, thereby helping in the negative thought process and the reasons behind that.

If you throw burning coal on your enemy, first the coal will burn your hands. The burning coal (bad feelings, emotions and memories) combusts your mind, making you sick; you are just hurting your mind and body in the process.

The mind is a fertile garden; as you sow, so shall you reap. What do we mean by 'sow'? If we entertain resentment in one aspect of life, say, towards their profession, their mind will continue to react resentfully towards that profession in the future too. Now, it's a matter of time before this resentment/frustration towards the profession starts affecting other daily activities of life, like driving a car, eating, reading the newspaper, etc. So, the mind will start proliferating this pattern of bad reactions and apply it to other aspects of life too. That is to say, it is similar to an avalanche that starts with only a small amount of snow rolling down a slope but quickly turns into a raging mass that has the capability to capture and move ice, rocks and trees.

In the fertile garden of the mind, both flowers and weeds grow. Flowers correspond to positive feelings like love, gratitude and compassion, and weeds correspond to negative feelings like ungratefulness, fear, greed, jealousy, frustration, discontentment, etc. Once the seeds are in the mind, these will start growing, and for this, you need to weed them out from time to time. Otherwise, your garden will be outgrown by weeds, consuming all the resources and overpowering the positive flowers.

There was a lady called Sudha. She was 'normal' initially but started becoming irritable because she was not getting the job she wanted. As time passed, she got married, but the problem remained and she was getting irritated with every aspect of her life. Soon, she got divorced; even though her husband was a good man, she was constantly irritated with him and everything else around her. The 'problem' was resolved only after she received professional treatment.

Another candidate, Ravi, was preparing for an exam, but in order to crack it, his frustration and anxiety pushed him to work really hard. It took him two attempts to clear the exam, but the anxiety had become generalized in his nature. As a result, this anxiety became a nagging issue every time he had to travel or when a senior questioned him or whenever he was stressed.

We need to focus on identifying the weeds (bad feelings) in our mind and pulling them out constantly—by forgiving and giving power to positive thoughts and cutting off the power supply of bad memories and feelings that silently kills you by affecting the neural networks.

We can see the same principle working in a different form for those who rely on religion. As they chant God's name in times of stress, with every repetition, they feel relaxed and contented as this relieves them of their uncertainties. With every chant, it is as if their God is directing their mind to strengthen the neural circuits related to love and security. With every chant, they are voluntarily triggering a set of neuron patterns in their minds that produces joy, relaxation and contentment. The more they do this, the stronger the pattern becomes. Over a period of time, the personality of such people becomes calm, secure and loving and they develop a stronger capacity to face tough mental situations in life. In the same way, meditation relaxes the mind and is considered to increase the production of the happy hormone, i.e. serotonin.

Exercise

So, what is the main feeling affecting your mind? Is it anger? Fear? Discontent? Irritation? Anxiety? Trust issues? Are you aiming for perfection? Are you constantly comparing yourself to others?

If you have identified the main feeling(s) affecting your mind, then write down how it all started. Try to recall the events surrounding the initiation of those feelings in your life.

Remember, our past is a combination of different events that may be completely different from or slightly related to each other.

The aim of this section is to make you cautious in the present and future by keeping you away from entertaining bad feelings so that they don't become an avalanche that starts silently but swiftly results in one or the other ailment. Although there's another way to combat the same—by writing your heart out.

WRITE YOUR HEART OUT

> *By putting pen to paper, we create a safe space for*
> *self-expression, self-reflection and self-discovery,*
> *leading to improved mental health and well-being.*

—Anonymous

Knowing about ourselves has been the most fundamental and difficult question we have encountered on the way to self-discovery and self-creation. One way to know yourself better is diary writing. It makes you emotionally organized, intelligent and stronger, makes your thought processes more reasonable and clearer, has healing powers and is a tool for learning new things about yourself. It will prioritize the issues in your life and planning will become a part of your personality, whether you re-read your diary or not.

You start getting clarity about yourself—what you have done, how past experiences have shaped you and most importantly, what you can be in the future if you know how to use the information correctly. Writing positive things will lead to more productive thoughts in your mind.

What to Write?

This book specifically deals with knowing your mental processes. When you need to improve, you need to give up many past beliefs and thoughts and negative experiences that are the mental barriers between you and your mental well-being. We need to unlearn/bypass old patterns of thought and learn new ones.

We need to write about how we reacted to certain situations and what we actually wanted to do, what kind of feelings we experienced in those situations, how we felt emotionally (were we worried or feeling anxious?) or whether it led us towards a mental ailment or psychological discomfort, and what physical symptoms started appearing or disappearing when a particular chain of thoughts was triggered.

A diary acts as a diagnosing tool for triggering a certain chain of thoughts and then helps in dissociating from negative emotions, dismantling older beliefs that are unhealthy for the mind and associating with positive emotions.

It is to be noted that writing bad experiences or negative articles, short stories, poems and then keeping the diary is as if you are associating these negative things with your subconscious mind. Basically, you're collecting poison and holding on to your diary/subconscious, rather than throwing them away/out of your head.

Take the example of a girl named Reena. She was suffering from a 'possession' disorder (temporary loss of the sense of individual identity).[65] There were many factors behind her

---

[65]Bhavsar, Vishal, Antonio Ventriglio, Dinesh Bhugra, 'Dissociative Trance and Spirit Possession: Challenges for Cultures in Transition', *Psychiatry*

medical situation but a strong trait of hers was that she was fond of writing negative anecdotes, negative interpretations of events, negative poems and negative fiction in her diary. She used to write down all her negative childhood events and experiences and poetry. In doing so, she was unintentionally reinforcing and reliving the bad experiences in her mind. She was giving negative affirmations to herself, and these give full concentration and experience to those feelings that you want to get rid of. For her, this may have been a way to vent her frustration, resentment or anger, but the result was actually the opposite, which she did not realize.

What to Keep, What to Throw Away?

Writing a diary as a passion but not knowing how to do it constructively can wreak havoc in your mind. So be careful. Diary writing is not about writing irrelevant stuff such as what you watched on TV today or how you made noodles.

There may be bad experiences or frustrations, resentful feelings towards someone or any kind of guilt that keeps nagging your mind and leads you to overthink or commands your complete attention. Such events can be written down on paper and then torn up and thrown away or burned (or you can also try flushing it down the toilet, à la Geet in *Jab We Met*). Doing such an activity will form a dissociation phenomenon in your mind about the things that are troubling you. This can be done 2–4 times, which will greatly diminish the negative intensity of thoughts in your mind. It's best to not write such thoughts/events unless you do it with the intention of turning

and Clinical Neurosciences, Vol. 70, No. 12, 2016, 551–559. https://doi. org/10.1111/pcn.12425.

things around (refer to the example of Arun below).

There is enough garbage around us and unknowingly we can be storing that garbage in our minds and make its presence strong by writing about it in a diary. Therefore, write only about your beautiful ideas and experiences, write optimistic poems and do what you like to do positively in your life. But remember, whatever you write in your diary is being put into your subconscious.

Points to remember

- Always write what good changes you want to see in yourself.
- Write about how your thought process works. For example, write about why you became angry when your parents asked you to do some work, or why you ignored them.
- Avoid writing negative narratives at all costs until you can introspect after writing.

Things to keep in mind while writing a diary

- Write down about things you are grateful for.
- What positive habits would you like to have?
- What are your positive plans for this week, this month, by the end of this year, next five years…?
- Do you have the habit of writing bad experiences in your diary?
- Do you write poems that are negative in tone?
- Do your children keep a diary? (If not, ask them to do so and teach them how to write.)

A Snapshot of My Diary

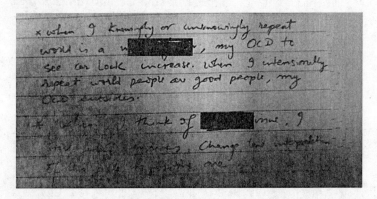

INVENT GOD FOR YOUR MIND'S SAKE

God is like oxygen, you can't see
Him but you can't live without Him.

—Anonymous

I am going to circle back to something that I have mentioned a number of times already, that our bodies and minds are not completely our own. While we inherited them from our ancestors, who evolved over millions of years, we also inherited the primitive emotion of fear, which is in consonance with nature and our changing environments and demands from time to time.[66] Those were perhaps times of more uncertainty and unpredictability when the primitive

---

[66]Betkowski, Bev, 'Why Phobias are Natural—and How to Overcome Them', *Medical Xpress*, 31 October 2019, https://medicalxpress.com/news/2019-10-phobias-naturaland.html. Accessed on 7 June 2023.

humans were fearful of animals as well as other problems such as droughts, floods and diseases (when no medical science had evolved). In particular, death is psychologically disruptive because it not only removes an individual member from our life but also potentially creates tension. Our mind has to bear uncertainties and has developed in those situations. So, it has certain needs that it wants to fulfil in order to sustain itself. One of those needs is to find certainty, and cling to someone/ something who/that always relieves the mind from fear, anxiety and misfortunes, thereby triggering positivity and relaxing it. This need of the mind forces humans to believe in a superpower, which can help us pass through all problems in life. This is relevant even today.

There is a need for God (or a superhuman being or someone whom we can believe in, say, some kind of higher power or spiritual force). As in the generations before us, we cannot deny this need of our minds on which it has always been relying for ages. Remember that we have inherited our body and mind from our ancestors and denying our minds and replacing it with logic that there is no God or higher power can make us subconsciously dissatisfied.

Just think—who do we chat with most of the time? Friends? Parents? No. It's ourselves. It's a constant internal dialogue or self-talk from 'I' to 'I'. There are various subjects that you can't share with someone, these may be your fears, insecurities and anxieties that you cannot alleviate with the help of other people around you. You are your best friend. Isn't it?

Because you chat so much with yourself, psychological pressure is created. But when you talk to others, including leaving an open space for God, in front of whom you place all your worries or emotions and your love, your mind is metaphorically insured from uncertainties and misfortunes of life. The mind requires a constant companion apart from itself, i.e. 'me'. Denying this is detrimental to the mind because, in doing so, you are closing a safety valve that will help you vent your mind's psychological waste. Secondly, when you keep on chatting with yourself, it creates psychological pressure on you. This is very normal. We are social creatures, which means our minds need to socialize. When we talk to someone else (be it other people or animals or God), we are being social. Our minds are satisfying their basic need to socialize. So, if your mind is trying to socialize with God too, or a similar higher power, won't that make you more courageous and robust?

Not believing in a higher power can make you more prone to stress factors; thus, for our mind's sake, either believe in God or invent a higher power that you can believe in, even if it's formless, and allow them to take care of you so that your mind can find a companion in times of distress.

Eminent sociologist Émile Durkheim theorized that humans invented totems (either an animal or any other natural object that was believed in by a particular culture to have spiritual importance and was embraced by such communities as their emblem) because of the uncertainties of life and nature and that these, later on, transformed into the concept of God.[67] Through this concept of God, humans are actually worshipping nature. So, you can invent a God, it could even be the all-powerful nature, and allow it to take care of you.

---

[67] Haekel, Josef, 'Totemism—A Short History of Totemistic Theory—Durkheim to Radcliffe-Brown', *Encyclopedia Britannica*, 8 September 2022, https://www.britannica.com/topic/totemism-religion/Durkheim-to-Radcliffe-Brown. Accessed on 7 June 2023.

Suppose a God-loving person (not fearing) chants the name of a specific god. As he loves God's name, with every repetition, he feels relaxed and contented. It relieves him of his uncertainties and brings joy to his mind and body. With every chant, he believes in Him more and reinforces the feeling in his mind, that is, he is directing his mind to strengthen the neural circuits related to love and security. With every chant, he voluntarily triggers specific neuron patterns in his mind, which produces joy. The more he does this, the more he makes this pattern strong. Over a long period of time, the nature of this person tends towards silence, security and love and they have a stronger capacity to face unpleasant mental situations in life as their mind is working on a love model, whether it is for God or some other positive concept.

We have already discussed the SNS (triggers fight-or-flight response) and the PNS (responsible for relaxation) in Chapter 1. God's name is the stimulator of PNS. It makes you feel relaxed, slows down the heart rate to normal, lets our intestines and glands work vibrantly and relaxes the sphincter muscles in the gastrointestinal tract.

Even meditation relaxes the mind and is said to increase the levels of serotonin, the happy hormone, in the body. Whenever you sit, stand or initiate/finish new work, just repeat God's name in a relaxed manner. Make it a habit.

MINDFUL APPRECIATION

> *Gratitude is not only the greatest of virtues,*
> *but the parent of all the others.*

> —Cicero

In school, our morning or pre-lunch prayers sought to inculcate the habit of thanksgiving among us so that we internalize this trait and reflect it in our attitude. According to various studies, children who are taught to be grateful are less prone to depression, anxiety and stress. This is why our elders tell us to be grateful for whatever we have; gratitude is a core cultural trait across the globe.

The human mind works on certain infallible rules. Whether you believe them or not, the rules have to be respected and followed; by not adhering, you are playing with your mind. Say, if you are standing at a height and if you fall, you will get hurt. Similarly, for the mind, one of the most important rules is being grateful for the things, events, situations, people and everything around you, or you will get hurt.

Humans are Dependent on Each Other

The feeling of gratitude is the most fundamental feeling. In ancient times, there were numerous uncertainties, threats, weather irregularities, diseases and natural calamities. So we had to depend on each other and stay in groups, thus making man a social being. Man has drawn security from this—both physically and psychologically. The sense of gratitude for human support has been ingrained into man's basic instinct, thereby making it a fundamental requirement of the mind. On the contrary, when we deny ourselves gratitude, it is like denying our mind to fulfil its fundamental needs, thus inviting trouble.

If you feel dissatisfied or disenchanted and think that the world is full of scoundrels and you don't feel gratitude for what you actually have, then that is akin to starving your mind. Soon, you will start drifting towards the path of mental unrest; whether this drifting will be slow or fast depends on various factors, most importantly on the current state of your situation and your past.

Not only does gratitude promote the larger good of society but it also binds the social order of bringing people closer to each other, which is good for your mental health too. It is such an important virtue that gratitude is called the mother of all virtues.

In a recent study, participants were divided into three groups. The first group was asked to write one letter of gratitude to another person each week for three weeks, whereas the second group was asked to write about their deepest thoughts and feelings about negative experiences.[68] The third group did not do any writing activity. When the findings were analysed, those who wrote gratitude letters[69] reported significantly better mental health than the other two groups.

Gratitude activates the production of serotonin, the happy hormone, an antidepressant neurotransmitter. By becoming more and more grateful for the things you have in your life, you gain strength; it becomes the maintenance factor for better mental health.

Technically, it is increasing the activity in the prefrontal

---

[68]Brown, Joshua, and Joel Wong, 'How Gratitude Changes You and Your Brain', *Greater Good Magazine*, 6 June 2017, https://greatergood.berkeley.edu/article/item/how_gratitude_changes_you_and_your_brain. Accessed on 12 May 2023.
[69]'Gratitude Letter', *Greater Good in Action*, https://ggia.berkeley.edu/practice/gratitude_letter. Accessed on 12 May 2023.

cortex of the brain—the dopamine neurotransmitter is in the mind; it is rewarding in nature and satisfies the brain's fundamental need to be grateful.

How to Go About It?

Just close your eyes and thank someone. When you silently introspect, a subtle pulse of pleasure and an expansive feeling of happiness runs throughout your body, thereby relaxing you. Let's see how this works.

The SNS and PNS come into play. The SNS makes you ready for the fight-or-flight response. Whenever your mind apprehends trouble, your blood flows faster, your heart rate increases and adrenaline and cortisol are released, thereby diverting the resources from the digestive system or other vital organs so that you can either fight or run away from danger. The PNS is the opposite; it relaxes you and the body focuses on repairing in a relaxed mode.

The PNS is triggered when you feel grateful. We have to stimulate it repeatedly. Whatever our age or gender, we always have the capability of changing ourselves as our brain is a wonderfully adaptive organ. That is, it has the ability to generate/alter neural networks through reorganization and growth. These changes can vary from discrete neuron pathways building novel connections to organized alterations like cortical remapping.[70] The more we use this feeling, the stronger the positive reaction within us; it's in our hands to make this feeling of being grateful stronger day by day by repeating it. This small feeling has immense power.

---

[70]Costandi, Moheb, *Neuroplasticity*, The MIT Press, Cambridge, Massachusetts, 2016.

Saying 'thank you', i.e. being grateful, lowers the threshold for being happy. We create self-goals that are too high for the time being and feel that we can be happy only after achieving those goals. This way, the mind is programmed and develops the habit to be happy only after an achievement, which may take months or years. Say, you will be happy after getting a good job, then buying a new car, then your children getting good grades, buying a bigger house, etc. Thus, **consistent postponing of the desire to be happy becomes detrimental to mental health** and a person becomes more prone to depression and anxiety.

General Practice

Positive feelings and thoughts mean positive present and future, and negative feelings and thoughts mean negative present and future. Gratitude unshackles us, frees us and cures us from toxic negative emotions. Don't deny your mind the basic need to be grateful; if you are not being grateful for smaller things in life, you are losing out on many opportunities; so, always find a reason to thank people, situations and places.

- Just think of people who are not as fortunate as you.
- Be grateful that you have a normal, functional body and organs.
- Think of those who were not born into a family like yours.
- Think of those who struggle to have two meals a day or those who neither go to school nor can read and write.

A shortcut to happiness lies in expressing gratitude in your mind itself. This will lead to higher levels of dopamine and stimulate the reward centre. Just close your eyes and thank everyone in your present and past. It does not require the presence of the other person—just say thank you silently to them, it will still positively add to your emotional health. Whether you thank in person or imagine yourself thanking someone, it will produce almost the same effect. You can say thank you for the sunlight or to God. This way, it will be easy to practice and you will feel relaxed.

Every person you met today/yesterday or at any point in time...recall their face and say thank you to them, whether they were good or bad. Recalling their faces will also improve your memory and strengthen your feeling of gratitude.

Point to ponder!

You will face resistance in saying 'thank you' to the people who have hurt you; *the more resistance you feel, the more you need healing.* This shows how strong your negative reactions are; they are silently damaging your mind and body without your knowledge. Change the negative image and feeling attached to them in your mind. *Neutralize them.*

As a human being, you cannot control your thoughts all the time; so, whenever thoughts that make you resentful, angry, envious or anxious surface, they put you in overthinking mode, and those thoughts subsequently get stuck in your mind. But, when you attach the feeling of forgiveness and gratitude for having learnt a new experience, then these bad thoughts will come and go instantly.

Benefits of Gratitude

- Lessens venomous emotions resulting from self and social comparisons.
- Lessens materialistic perceptions.

- The repetition of gratitude reduces the craving for things we don't need (but it does not make your aspirations less); it is no surprise that a grateful person is happier and more content with life and less miserable and less tense.
- Cultivates pro-social behaviour, it helps in tackling stress.
- Increases self-esteem.
- Enhances access to positive memories and helps in switching to a positive thought process.
- Makes the mind feel secure, increases compassion and inspires ethical and proper behaviour.

Curiosity and Wonder

We are all born curious, but only a small number of people remain curious for a lifetime.

—Eraldo Banovac

As we age, we generally lose interest in doing new things and assume that we already know and have experienced it all. This sabotages our curiosity. This assumption is like a gun that backfires as it closes the window of our flexibility, receptivity and adaptability to new ideas. Do you remember how you were more alive, creative and enthusiastic in your childhood? Your learning capability was also high, but as you kept growing, you became narrower in your approach and crystallized in your thinking. When your mind is open to options, it's good for your mental health. Your mind becomes stale when thinking becomes narrower.

The brain is a miser in using energy resources, i.e. it tries to save energy all the time, something that we already discussed in Chapter 4. It locks up its functionality to rediscover and tries to impose already known habits, biases and prejudices on people and situations. So, we always have to keep an open mind and not form strong, unchanging opinions quickly as this may be indicative of some underlying mental health issues.

Suppose you are inclined towards right-wing politics; then, you become open to left-wing and centrist political views too. Don't suffocate your mind. Be more open and tolerant to all classes and communities and respect other people's opinions, even if you don't agree with them. Becoming adamant, aggressive and anxious with age are symptoms that you will soon pay the price for in terms of your mental peace and health. So, focus on the wonders of life and nature because if you start closing down your windows of learning and boast/believe that you have already experienced everything in life, you will surely suffocate yourself. It's like the silkworm that spins cocoons but dies within its creation.

The more curious and enthusiastic you are and the more you wonder about things, the more neurons and neuron patterns are produced and replaced in your brain. It is one of the best things that you can add to the health of your brain. And the one who lacks curiosity is surely going to deteriorate faster as the rate of formation of new neuron patterns will slow down substantially.

You can amplify curiosity, enthusiasm and wonder by making small changes in life, such as taking a new route to the market, opting to use the bicycle to roam around, exploring new paths on morning walks, trying to read a new genre of literature or watching videos on new topics that might interest you. Try to wonder how complex and also how simple everything is. Try new things. Try to play a new sport whenever you get the chance. The crux of this section is to start exploring things with curiosity and wonder.

The shortest possible path to being creative is to keep thinking about everything happening around you as a creative process. So, practice this approach in your mind for some time every day, until it becomes an automatic process in your subconscious mind. Sometimes, we may become too negative. We keep on watching and interpreting things in a divisive manner. Our brain also has demands, for example, some psychiatric patients are asked to perform creative activities like making a paper craft, which stimulates the dopamine receptors. Similarly, you can pursue a hobby. The basic premise of pursuing a hobby is that it makes you creative and enthusiastic apart from making you wonder about the new things that you could explore. You will start seeing the benefits of viewing everything creatively, which will subsequently benefit your conscious and subconscious thinking processes.

What does it mean to see everything as a creative process? It means that you are now seeing everything—whether it is cleaning your bedsheets, arranging your books or anything else you can think of—as being creative in nature. That is to say, every process that is happening right now will act in a positive way. This is also a very basic instinct of the mind—that it needs to create.

Think about plants. They are creative as they take up nutrients from the soil and carbon dioxide from the environment, grow in size, produce flowers, give out oxygen and provide eatables for humans and animals.

Think about your car. It is used for transportation, made up of different materials and composed of different types of metals that are used to make it workable. Think of all the processes that resulted in the making of the chassis, doors, seats, wiring and glasses, all of which came together to form the car.

Exercise

The motive is to think creatively, so that your mind enjoys the pleasure of having achieved something constructive and creative, even if not physically but at least mentally.

Think about cycle making. Think about how the postal system works. Think how the vegetables growing in a field reach your plate. Think about the political system—how the people vote, how the votes are counted, how constructively the system is designed—see creativity in everything.

Take as many examples as you can take and let your mind start thriving on the creative feelings that are good for your brain's health.

Now let us target those issues about which you think negatively. List them as follows:

Politics: If you don't like the present politics of any nation, think creatively and positively about how you can change it or even detach yourself from the topic.

Religion and community: If there is oppression, your creative and positive thinking about how to change this will help you in uniting and reorganizing your community.

Write about the above creatively and positively.

Do the same thing for processes that are very complex, like those of nature, like the biological processes behind the blooming of flowers, how the universe works, etc. In other words, give your mind a dose of wonder, just like you used to think curiously and wonder about everything in your childhood.

11

Parenting in the New Age

In all this world there is nothing so beautiful as a happy child.

—L. Frank Baum

Children are natural in their behaviour, which helps us in understanding the underlying behaviour pattern of all humans. As they grow up, they learn cognitive skills, attach meanings to their actions, learn to act and react to their environment, learn languages and so forth. The family teaches them to socialize and they are ready to deal with the world. Their natural behaviour is covered up by their social behaviour.

Children have fewer negative experiences and resentments, frustrations, guilt or anger when compared to grown-ups who have willy-nilly collected many negative experiences and beliefs throughout their lives. Because their minds are clear and enthusiastic, children are creative and receptive to new learning. This is a lesson for adults that if our negative baggage becomes less, we too can be very creative and receptive and our performance will see a transformation. When we become passionate and excited about learning again, the formation of dendrites and synapses takes place in the same way it happens in children. The more passionate we are, the better our mind will respond.

LAUGH LIKE A CHILD

> *To weep is to make less the depth of grief.*
>
> —William Shakespeare

> *Do not apologize for crying.*
> *Without this emotion, we are only robots.*
>
> —Elizabeth Gilbert

It has been categorically found that the chemicals that build up in our body during emotional stress can be shed through tears. It is a great stress buster. We feel lighter when we weep. This is the natural way for the body to vent and de-stress. You can see this in the natural behaviour of infants who don't yet speak a language but vent or show their unrest through crying. But as we grow, social pressures suppress the need to cry, mostly for males. Females can still retain a balance and calmness of mind as they do vent their suppressed feelings through weeping. Unreleased stress can increase the risk for the heart and brain and cause other mental ailments. Suppressed sorrow always spills over, mostly in the form of rudeness or violence. We have already mentioned the mental traps in Chapter 1.

We are already aware that laughter is contagious. If one child is laughing, the other child will also start laughing. The same works for adults. It is important to mention here that the mirror neurons in the brain are activated, which are responsible for this type of response.[71] So it's always better to

---

[71]Lubejko, Susan, 'The Neuroscience of Laughter', *Neuwrite*, 23 August 2018, https://neuwritesd.org/2018/08/23/the-neuroscience-of-laughter/. Accessed on 7 June 2023.

stay in jovial company.

Crying stimulates the PNS, which is responsible for relaxing the body. Tears stimulate the release of oxytocin and endogamous opioids made by the body. So crying or weeping is nothing to be ashamed of; do it whenever you feel like venting and cleanse your mind.

BEHAVIOURAL DISORIENTATION IN CHILDREN

How do we identify children who do not behave normally? We are looking specifically at children and youth between the ages of 5 and 20 years here. The causes could be mental retardation or harsh parenting that affects the psyche of children who could have some psychological/psychiatric illness.

Children not only learn from their family members' verbal directions but also by observing them, which is called observational learning. For example, if the parent is obsessed with maintaining cleanliness (repetitively cleaning hands, rearranging things precisely, etc.), has antagonistic or awful thoughts about losing control over others, has the habit of overthinking, has violent thoughts or is excessively religious, then the child may start exhibiting similar behavioural responses, even though not as much as their parents. Behavioural disorders may start if they remain under pressure (regarding studies, etc.) or are facing social or some form of emotional or physical abuse. Some children develop an inclination for drugs, alcohol and smoking, which may cause further deterioration in their behaviour.

Other reasons can be genetic. Social media is the new concern with wide ramifications; children are playing violent games that affect their mental health. Chatting with strangers whose motives are unknown and craving attention from social media rather than interacting with real people are other manifestations of behavioural disorders.

ADHD is a chronic medical condition that affects children and continues into adulthood. It includes problems such as difficulty in focussing or poor attention, hyperactivity and impulsive behaviour. I am mentioning ADHD only to inform readers but it is up to the paediatrician or family doctor or specialist to identify the problem. Some children may show symptoms of depression or they try to become the devil themselves, always wanting attention by being involved in nefarious acts.

Other symptoms include constant or increasing behaviour of aggression and bullying parents, siblings and other children; throwing things around at home; lying, bunking school and moving around in the city (some children step out of their houses to roam silently and none of their family members know about it); running away from home for some days; answering back on every issue just for the sake of hurting or intentionally disagreeing; suffering from mood swings and low self-esteem; and using abusive words and refusing to stop, even when they are being corrected or punished. A child may also have issues like telling lies, committing small thefts or becoming violent and creating drama when confronted with something disagreeable to them.

In such cases, professional treatment becomes necessary, and the parents may consult the family doctor or counsellor who would be able to diagnose the cause and take steps to remedy the situation, even with medication that mellows the child's anti-social behaviour.

If such behavioural disorientations are not taken care of at an early stage, children may turn out to be anti-social adults. Criminal behaviour, drug addiction and divorce rate can also be high among such people and they will be more prone to mental ailments, personality disorders like narcissism and other chronic diseases that substantially bring down the quality of life.

Proper diagnosis by a professional not only involves the child but also the family members who may be responsible for the child's behaviour. It includes family therapy wherein all family members are made to sit and reason why the child's behaviour is the way it is. Problems can either be because of harsh parenting or over-pampering by parents wherein the child may show a poor level of emotional intelligence.

Many problems can be resolved by increasing the time of quality interaction between the child and parents.

DIGITAL AGE AND NEW CHALLENGES

Technological developments have psychological implications for growing children. The advent of the digital age, marked by the proliferation of online and offline games, mobile phones and other gadgets, along with our increased exposure to digital products and services have taken a toll on children's mental health.

It is always advisable that children below the age of 3 years should be prevented from screen exposure. Of course, many parents will complain that their children do not eat food without looking at the TV/mobile. Children emotionally bargain with their parents to do so; otherwise, they throw tantrums. Such exposure may hamper their cognitive development as it interferes with their attention span, which is lowered with constant use of these devices. Parents must be strict enough to refuse to give gadgets, such as phones, to children at a young age and stand their ground. If the child asks for other things (say, a toy) in a peaceful and composed way, the parent could consider allowing their use but only for a short time.

Ideally, children should not be given phones until they have passed out from high school. However, even if they are given a phone at this stage, there should be no lock as that would allow them to create a private social media account without your awareness. The downside of giving your child a phone to stay connected to you is that they become vulnerable to unknown dangers. Children need assistance and proper guidance from parents to identify whom to talk to or how to avoid bad company. It is the same thing as giving them social media accounts with a password so that they have private space that may turn out to be harmful. Strangers can post all sorts of vulgar or violent images, asking your kids to share their pictures, tracking your children or asking for family details, exploiting your children emotionally to a point where it could become difficult for everyone in your family.

Children Glued to Computers

Children who are addicted to gadgets can be classified into three broad categories (this is also applicable to college students).

Interactors: Those who are hyperactive on social media, such as sharing images, activities, constant updates and writing/copy-pasting poetry, want constant attention as there is a need to get approval, while for many it is just for the sake of attention whether sharing positive or negative content. Because of their overindulgence in social media, they drift from reality to a world of fake interactions. The time they could spend on real social interaction and mental activities is overtaken by time on social media.

Watchers: Those who are mute spectators, are overtly curious and therefore put all their energy into exploring different but non-relevant content on the internet throughout the night, thereby disturbing their sleep cycle. The screens emit light that reduces the secretion of melatonin by the pineal gland, which induces sleep, and hence, their studies and schooling are impacted. In the long run, they become prone to anxiety and depression, lowering their quality of life. It is not good that you get addicted to this type of activity when you are expected to follow your school curriculum, putting you on the path of mental illness. With addiction, the reward centre of the brain gets stimulated, which secretes dopamine, and there develops a constant vicious loop of anxiety and unhappiness, followed by an urge to get external sources of dopamine. The strong urge turns into addiction like any other drug.

There are also 'roasters' on social media, who use all sorts of foul language, legitimizing the use of abuses and hurling them at others. Roasting, thus, becomes a source of learning abuses for children as they have millions of followers and are eulogized for their content, thus establishing a negative reference group for children.

Gamers: Those who are constantly involved in online/offline games—including violent ones—not only on holidays but all through the night, thereby affecting their sleep cycle, schooling and studies. Such children are the worst affected, for they get so obsessed that sometimes they need to be hospitalized.

PROBLEMS CAUSED BY BAD PARENTING

The usual method parents apply is to negatively motivate their children by comparing them with other children. However, such comparisons are a blow to the self-esteem of children. It may motivate them but it leads to more damage in the form of envying others and resentment towards parents and the child goes into a loop of self-deprecation. Self-deprecation is an extremely negative trait wherein no outsider but their affirmations about 'not being good enough' is destroying the psyche of a child, and this becomes an integral part of the child's personality. The child keeps repeating and self-suggesting throughout their lives, thus turning themselves into a prisoner of their minds.

Sometimes the parents' behaviour need not be biased, but the child may still perceive it as biased. The child who has become better in terms of achievements gets more attention from the family. Also, in a patriarchal system, the male child gets to explore better opportunities for higher studies than a female child. This induces low self-esteem and a vicious loop of self-deprecation for the girl child.

Sometimes, children are brought up in an overprotective environment. Their freedom is curbed and exposure to the outside world is minimized. This overprotection is due to the insecurity of the parents that their children would be harmed or that they would go off track, but when the line between protection and overprotection fuses, it inflicts harm on the child's overall personality. The parents' insecurity may be due to their insecurity and improper socialization while growing up, or an implicit trust deficit with respect to the outer world. It is how similar values are transferred to the children as well. This is how the transmission of values, biases and prejudices takes place. Even after marriage, such children are over-dependent on their parents, and then the parents' interference due to their insecurity messes with the married life of their children, or these children don't even get married sometimes. Rather than the children taking decisions for their actions, the parents take decisions for them. Such children, when they grow up, need constant validation for their actions from their parents. When overly protected, such children find it difficult to make friends. A smaller friend circle may mean less exposure due to a trust deficit regarding the world. The courage to take decisions diminishes and a habit of blaming others develops. Blaming is the way in which they reduce their psychological stress and don't take responsibility. Sometimes, they become over-responsible, putting them under huge psychological pressure, because they want to be a 'good boy' or 'good girl' to receive validation.

When children are ignored in their growing years, the nature of their relationship with their parents—usually fuelled by warmth and care—changes, and so does their perspective of themselves and the outer world. They may consider the outer world as full of deceitful people, or they land up in a self-deprecation loop resulting in lower self-esteem or aggressive behaviour. The worldview of parents, however it be, usually gets reflected in their children. The children in return may develop a superiority complex, which may be a reaction to their inferiority complex. Their inner and outer selves are different. They play dual roles, spending more energy fighting their own inferiority complexes from the inside while exhibiting a superiority complex to the outside world. They start becoming misfits in the world, thereby spoiling their personal and professional relationships in the same way as the overprotected children. Depending upon the degree of abuse a child has undergone in the formative years, they may become irresponsible and anti-social, inflict violence on others and justify mala fide and anti-social actions.

Backbenchers in school usually demand attention. Care and validation are basic requirements of every child. Those who are not so good in academics resort to attention-seeking measures such as creating a ruckus in class, hooting and harassing other children. John Bowlby, a British psychologist and psychiatrist, explains in his Attachment Theory the four types of personalities that are formed depending on the relationship of a child with the primary caregiver (usually one parent).[72] This personality type also determines the relationship with the spouse and their general behaviour.

TYPES OF ATTACHMENTS

Secure attachment: In this case, the child shares a secure and confident relationship with the primary caregiver (usually mother and/or father). Gaining the trust of the caregiver is easy in such a case; hence the child's social skills are good as they received proper attention. This also means that the child's self-esteem is high and that they are stable and optimistic.

Insecure attachment[73]: This is of three types. Such personalities are less curious, and gaining trust is difficult as

[72]Mcleod, Saul, 'John Bowlby Attachment Theory', *Simply Psychology*, 4 June 2023, https://www.simplypsychology.org/bowlby.html. Accessed on 8 June 2023.
[73]Bottaro, Angelica, 'How to Heal an Insecure Attachment Style', *Verywell Health*, 20 April 2022, https://www.verywellhealth.com/insecure-attachment-5220170. Accessed on 8 June 2023.

they were made to feel insecure by their primary caregiver (unintentionally). Such children tend to have poor social skills, and they have a problem making friends. This type of attachment is common.

Anxious/ambivalent attachment: This happens when a child becomes wary of strangers and suffers from separation anxiety when their parents leave. So as they grow up, they become moody, clingy and unpredictable. They expect validation from the spouse that was denied to them in their childhood by the primary caregiver.

Avoidant/dismissive attachment: This happens when a child does not seek comfort from their parents. Such children, on growing up, are less inclined to share their feelings with anyone. This may be because the child may have sought attention previously but didn't get it most of the time, or got the desired attention in the form of harsh treatment. So they start hiding feelings and develop low self-esteem.

Disorganized attachment: This happens when a child avoids parents out of fear, resulting from growing up in an insecure environment. They start feeling that they do not deserve love, like children who have grown up away from their parents. As an adult, such people avoid intimacy.

In all these cases, the care that a child could not get from their primary caregivers is later expected as adults from the spouse. This also shows that we can be considerate of our spouse rather than behaving according to their personality type, which is an outcome of our upbringing.

ATTENTION DEFICIT HYPERACTIVITY DISORDER IN ADULTS

Not only children but adults are also prone to ADHD, especially those who have suffered from it as a child. In some cases, ADHD gets normalized with increasing age, but for others, it remains the same or reduces with age. Family history is also a cause wherein a parent or an extended family member has been afflicted with ADHD.

AUTISM IN CHILDREN

Autistic children do not differentiate much between parents and strangers. They find it difficult to emotionally mingle with or relate to people. Their verbal and other responses are slow and they ask illogical questions and show repetitive responses to some questions. They also have poor or irregular non-verbal communication. Only professionals can diagnose and treat them. Such children have difficulty making friends.

LABELLING YOUR KIDS

Parents and teachers should refrain from labelling their kids even if they are angry or simply expressing their affection. Calling children stupid or dumb or describing them in disparaging words could put them down. You never know how deep the stone goes when you throw it into a river. Children may unknowingly absorb the words and start considering them to be true. Rather, you should use words that invoke courage and boost their self-esteem.

NEVER JUSTIFY YOUR CHILD'S WRONGDOINGS

Sometimes, parents justify the wrongdoings of their children. Shielding children in such cases would only lead them towards a darker road, attracting punishment and even imprisonment in some cases. For example, a father tried to shield his adolescent boy's act of violence at a police station. This particular boy was always more daring than all of us. But when he indulged in eve teasing, the girl went to the police station. Nevertheless, the boy's father defended his son. There were also other instances when the father shielded his son from being called to task for certain actions. One day, we all came to know that he fought with someone and the other guy died of wounds. Now this friend is in jail for life. He was just 24 years old when he was convicted. So, the lesson is, never side with your children if they do any wrong as this may put them on the wrong path in life.

CHILDREN SEE CHILDREN DO

Remember that children usually are a replica of their parent's personality traits. Many of their fundamental traits come from their parents because 'children see children do'. The actions performed by parents and the people around them are consciously and subconsciously copied by children, which is also known as observational learning. If parents remain anxious, children may also become anxious; if parents are complaining all the time, children may think and act like that; if parents are fighting, children may become violent or timid.

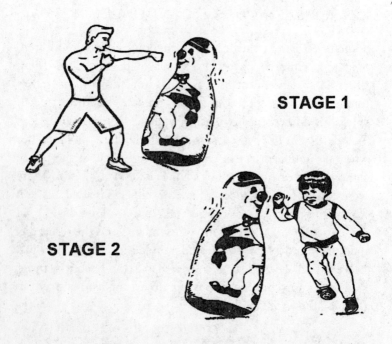

STAGE 1

STAGE 2

Children see children do: Children imitating their parents' behaviour

Each child is unique. Just scoring well in academics is not one's insurance to be successful in life. If you have kids who are not so keen on studies, encourage them to do so, but don't pressurize them as you never know you may push the child to such an extent that you may lose them. **Not being good in academics is as normal as being good.** We can still identify many people in our circle who were below average in academics, but earn far better than us and are more successful according to societal parameters today. We need to help our children grow up to become happy and successful people, not necessarily academicians.

Children failing in exams or entrance tests can be a blessing in disguise as a child can be trained to handle failures and that too under one's able guidance. Success and failure, ups and downs are a part and parcel of life. It is better for children to face and learn from their failures as early as possible. Failing should not be taken as an end; it is just a start, a new inning and it gives us time to fix our wrong habits. There are examples of children we read in newspapers who scored well all through childhood but couldn't handle failure in adult life to the point of contemplating or even committing suicide. So, you need to decide—do you want a reformed and courageous kid or no kid?

Be Frank with Your Kids

The youth are like unguided missiles; you have to keep track of them. Parents should be frank with their children, especially during adolescence, so that they can keep track of their activities and guide them in a convincing way rather than forcefully. Modern societal values are democratic; hence, forcing your children will backfire immediately or in the near future. When children are not handled in a tactful way, they become unreceptive or may even turn against you.

Let Your Children Chase their Dreams

Many parents try to live their dreams through their children, thus setting the same targets for them as they would do for themselves. Each child has a unique mindset and worldview informed by their inclinations and experiences. We can only suggest and give children the opportunities that they could explore. Just introspect...without knowing your child's desires, are you making them live out *your* definition of life and career?

Time moves fast. Parents must focus on upcoming trends while considering possible career opportunities for their children. They can then discuss these with their children who are about to start their careers. Sometimes, parents keep pushing their children to take up jobs that are presently popular but could become irrelevant in the future.

Grandparents and grandchildren complement each other. If they stay together, grandparents can impart moral values. Here, grandparents have to keep in mind that there is going to be a generation gap, so they (grandparents) should keep ahead of their time. They must develop interests, be tech-savvy and keep educating themselves on new technologies so that their grandchildren can relate to them. Also, grandparents act as a buffer in the family and they can be very good friends with the children.

Children believe what they see; they must be told not to take movies seriously, and that they are only for entertainment. Watching extra-marital affairs, unrealistic love stories and crime and nefarious actions lead to instant gratification, making their minds believe these things. Rather, children should be encouraged to read; consider creating a library at home. Reading good books shapes the mind and instils positive beliefs and values.

Parents and their children have totally different mindsets, so it's not surprising that parents sometimes don't know how to handle certain situations. It is normal for parents to opt for counselling and take their children to counsellors as well. We must not get concerned about the so-called social stigma around counselling and go beyond our own biases and fears to seek help. In today's complex and heterogeneous environment, parents may not be able to professionally handle the challenges faced by their children. Children are the assets of a family; we should not hesitate if we need to take professional help.

If the parents are suffering from certain chronic physical or mental ailments, children should also be made aware of the preventive measures to avoid these ailments. As children inherit their bodies from their parents, the probability of these ailments being passed on to them is high. It is always best to adopt a healthy lifestyle, as I have stated throughout this book. For example, parents who are suffering from a cardiac issue must make their children aware of lifestyle changes to prevent them from developing the same health problems in the future.

Don't give your kids all the luxuries of life, even if you can afford to do so. Give them targets, which if met, will be rewarded. Set practical targets for success. Using the stick policy should be avoided with older kids. Motivation is better than using pressure or fear to make a child work. Otherwise, the child will associate the thought of studying with fear and anxiety.

Children's communication skills are also affected when they are not encouraged to talk by the family or are snubbed for raising irrelevant issues, which leads to lower self-esteem. The right way must be to encourage them to speak and even ask for their opinions and correct them if required. This becomes an inclusive process of interaction that will reflect in a child's personality when they go to school or college or face the world later on. They will be instilled with democratic values.

EFFECTS OF CHILDHOOD TRAUMA

Addiction can be related to childhood experiences that become part of an adult's personality. According to Gabor

Maté, a Canadian physician, addiction can be attributed to childhood trauma or trauma during adulthood that has now become a part of our personality. Maté's approach to addiction focuses on the trauma his patients have suffered and looks to address this in their recovery. He defines addiction as any behaviour or substance that a person uses to relieve pain in the short term, but which leads to negative consequences in the long term.[74] The addictive substances act as painkillers to bring down the pain inflicted subconsciously by bad experiences. Emotional pain and actual physical pain activate the same part of the brain. So, emotional rejection of the child or adult (by parents or a peer group or lover) is a larger trigger for addictive behaviour. Such vulnerable individuals resort to their addiction because they discover that the addictive substance/behaviour provides short-term relief and comfort from their suffering.[75]

Further, making a child feel guilty or shameful as a technique is also detrimental to the child. For example, parents often say that they have sacrificed so much and given the child way better resources than they had received from their parents and yet the child is not successful. This kind of behaviour inflicts feelings of guilt and shame on the child, which will only discourage them. When the child absorbs this, they go into a loop of self-deprecation. When self-deprecation

---

[74]Lavitt, John, 'Addiction is a Response to Childhood Suffering: In Depth with Gabor Maté', *ICPPD*, 1 March 2016, https://icppd.com/addiction-is-a-response-to-childhood-suffering-in-depth-with-gabor-mate/. Accessed on 8 June 2023.

[75]Heshmat, Shahram, 'Why Drugs Can Be So Appealing to Some People', *Psychology Today*, 26 March 2019, https://www.psychologytoday.com/us/blog/science-choice/201903/why-drugs-can-be-so-appealing-some-people. Accessed on 19 June 2023.

starts, then the child doesn't need other people to put them down, the belief system will produce such feelings and thoughts, and throughout their life, they will feel ashamed of themselves. This mental process becomes automatic, thereby leading to lower self-esteem, and triggers various other issues in the cognitive behaviour of a child.

Some children always remain anxious and cannot relax. Parental behaviour like constantly reminding children of limited time and to study, otherwise they will fail, etc. results in the child internalizing the limitations of time, which may lead to constant anxiety. This, in turn, may lead to a child having generalized anxiety disorder later in life.

Some parents don't give their children adequate attention. For example, a parent may validate and encourage a child at one point, but afterwards, start demeaning them. By behaving this way, the parent is programming their child in such a way that the child needs constant validation from that parent and loses the courage to take independent decisions. Such children grow up and need similar demands from their spouses too, which, if fulfilled, helps in addressing the issue; otherwise, they end up making a mess of their lives. All the above has been summed up in a beautiful poem titled *Children Learn What They Live* by Dorothy Law Nolte.[76]

---

[76]Law Nolte, Dorothy, 'Children Learn What They Live', *Children Learn What They Live*, 1972, https://childrenlearnwhattheylive.com/. Accessed on 8 June 2023.

12

Ageing with Hope and Finding Joy

Wrinkles should merely indicate where smiles have been.

—Mark Twain

Youth and middle age are usually defined as the most productive periods of our lives, when we are more resourceful and capable of making meaningful contributions. But, we sometimes wonder how the years and our life pass us by in front of our eyes. Time flies and life just goes on. Recently, there has been growing speculation that the best period in a human's life is not in their 20s and 30s but their 60s and 70s.[77] Let's see how. In the 20–35 age group, we need to score high in studies as there is family pressure, peer pressure, pressure to make our careers and then ample exposure to go astray or be distracted by some love affair, parents' expectations, stress when your partner has issues with your parents and the pressure to be independent and rear children.

When we talk of old age, life is almost or already settled. You have had a career, you are retired or retiring, your children are grown up and have started becoming independent and at

---

Hill, Amelia, 'Could Your 60s and 70s be the Best Decades of Life?', *The Guardian*, 20 February 2017, https://www.theguardian.com/membership/2017/feb/20/retirement-60s-best-decade-life-ageing-joy. Accessed on 8 June 2023.

later stages, you become a grandparent or a great-grandparent. You have seen life, gained much experience, have a clearer thought process than ever before, have priorities, understand more closely the meaning of life and know where your energy should be invested to derive maximum benefit. You are more accepting of what others say and are more capable of taking your decisions in life. For example, the prime minister of our country, Narendra Modi, is a septuagenarian (in his 70s), and one cannot question his energy; his cabinet comprises more than 60 ministers, many Noble Prize winners aged above 60, and chief executive officers of various multinational corporations. There are many inspiring stories of older people who, with talent, perseverance and experience, have achieved wonders. For example, Isaac Newton was working enthusiastically at the age of 85. Socrates learned to play music at the age of 80. Michelangelo painted some of his greatest works at the age of 81.

After retirement, my uncle set up an academy and is now running a large judiciary coaching institute in the city. My grandmother at above 90 years could easily go up and down 2-3 storeys easily, had a sharp memory and behaved like she was 70 years old. Recently, a viral video of a man aged above 90 years skydiving gave me goosebumps. Videos of the famous actor Milind Soman's elderly mother doing push-ups are quite an inspiration too.

Life is not just about discovering life but courageously creating it. As you are more of a free bird than ever before, it's time to fly even higher. It is a G(old) Age to put your energies into your passions and a big opportunity to give back to yourself and society at large.

The common myth about Gold Age men and women is that they have worked very hard in their life, so now they are retired. Sometimes I feel the government should change the word 'retirement'. It is a misnomer that our Gold folks take too seriously to heart. They are of the firm belief that now they will take rest and enjoy life by doing very little or no work. Here's the problem. When your mind remains young, you remain young—by not doing the creative work you like every day, you are stalling the process of new neuron patterns being generated. Not working creatively with your mind will make it go in the reverse direction and result in its deterioration. You might rapidly become mentally and physically weak. When you are curious and passionate about learning, the generation of new dendrites and synapses takes place in the same way it does in children.[78] So, take this seriously—**engage in creative work every day by following your passion.**

The above also breaks the myth that with ageing you get irreversible memory loss; however, it is a known fact now that it all depends on your mindset and how you treat yourself.

A purposeful life is a hopeful life. If you are feeling hopeless, then chalk out a plan about what you are going to do in the short or long term (personal plans as well as those attached to some form of social work). One of the rules of sustaining a healthy mind is to attach it to social goals, which is actually an inbuilt need.

Write here if you don't maintain a diary. Don't read this casually—think, write and move forward; consider this your workbook.

---

[78]Klemm, William R., 'How Does Learning Change the Brain?', *Psychology Today*, 7 January 2020, https://www.psychologytoday.com/us/blog/memory-medic/202001/how-does-learning-change-the-brain. Accessed on 8 June 2023.

What are you going to do?

This week

This month

This year

In the next 5, 10, 20 or 40 years

Now, in your mind, repeat these targets that you have jotted down, and when you feel low, recall the purpose and you will feel reinvigorated. Your goals should be practical and achievable. You must always be ready with a Plan B; if anything fails, you may become purposeless and can still go into a loop of hopelessness. Make passionate plans and execute them.

We must take care of our physical health as that blows us up at a psychological level. Though medical science now ensures a longer life than before, our food pattern in the last 20-30 years has changed tremendously, which is a matter of concern. Adopting a nutritional lifestyle strategy is recommended. We must follow a balanced diet suitable for our changing bodies. Search for and join credible health groups or consult qualified dietitians who will subconsciously lead you to adapt a healthy lifestyle. Take care of your mental health, which we generally ignore in our present times, especially when our partner passes away or we suffer from some other irrevocable loss. So, it's very important to hook up with work that you are passionate about, not just part-time but full-time. Also, some form of physical exercise is also important for your mental well-being.

Once we hit 60, it's crucial that we remember that it is not an age for retirement per se (nature/biology doesn't recognize this), but only the beginning of a new inning with more clarity, experience and mental peace than ever. We must stay in touch with changing technology; we should remain enthusiastic about the emerging new media so that we remain ahead or on a par with the younger generations. Be open to new ideas, the world changes fast these days and getting along with the world is necessary. We must be interactive and expressive—that will really do the trick. Life is always about learning new things and it stops when you put a barrier for yourself and don't change your mindset with the changing times. Try to change—you will feel great. You are lucky to get to the Gold Age, nature wants you to enjoy it—just look around you and see how many have already said goodbye to the world before reaching your age. How lucky you are to still be alive!

> *Animals are such agreeable friends—they ask no questions, they pass no criticisms.*
>
> —George Eliot

Another beautiful thing we can do is interact with an animal so that we can feel joy. My family didn't prefer having a dog around when we adopted one, but now, he is the most important member of our family. When you have a pet, your motivation and compassion increase. The levels of the cortisol hormone associated with stress are reduced and happy hormones like serotonin increase. Of course, it is preferable that the breed of the dog is friendly and docile, which can keep the family's mood up.

> *There is a huge amount of suffering that is generated not by the actual challenges in life but by the fictitious problems that the mind generates.*
>
> —Eckhart Tolle

One of the most crucial aspects that is detrimental to our life is the assumption that we have seen all of life and know everything. This assumption usually backfires as it closes the window of flexibility and adaptability to new ideas. This severely kills our enthusiasm and passion for life. Do you feel like you are heading towards a narrow approach and crystallized views so much so that the space your mind needs is decreasing?

We have already mentioned how the brain tries to save energy to avoid similar situations, especially if they are perceived as dangerous or harmful. This is how habits, prejudices, biases, stereotypes and patterns or generalized views are formed. The brain, as mentioned earlier, avoids rediscovering the same things again. It locks up its function to rediscover; therefore, it tries to impose already known habits, biases and prejudices on people and situations. So, always be open to new experiences no matter how old you are.

> If you are old and need to start psychiatric medication, you must note that at times, bodies react to medicines and patients feel too lethargic in the beginning, because of which many end up not taking their medicine(s). It's better to consult your doctor again and ask for a lighter dose or a change in medication.
>
> Older people usually witness the onset of dementia, so it's always better to keep a close watch on their body clock and make their schedules according to the natural circadian rhythm. This means they should wake up with the rising of the sun, and sleep properly at night.

Living with an open mind and considering multiple ways and options is good for your mental health. The mind becomes stale with narrower approaches. If you subscribe to 'right wing' ideology, then become open to the political views of the left and the centre, as more prejudgements, prejudices, biases and grudges hold you back by not allowing your mind to thrive. These biases, prejudices and grudges are the walls that are not letting you think outside your mental prison. Again, go outside, something may have changed. Let's not suffocate the mind. Therefore, the process of neuroplasticity in the brain slows down as you don't learn new things and don't stay enthusiastic. Be more open and tolerant to all classes, communities and genders, and respect other people's opinions even if you don't agree. Becoming adamant and aggressive are symptoms that you are doing the opposite of what the healthy mind needs to do. So, focus on the wonders of life and nature because if you start closing your windows of learning in the assumption that you have experienced life and boast about it, it will surely suffocate you.

The other crucial factor that makes old people think negatively is the general weakening of the physical body. This factor reaffirms the idea that they are getting old, and soon, they start thinking and worrying about memory loss and other physical issues that may develop in the near future. This accelerates the problem. Their self-conception makes them age faster. We have seen how many old people are achieving more excellence in what they do at their present than at their young ages. Age is a question of mind over matter—if you don't mind it, it doesn't matter. Some healthy oldies consider themselves to be in a better mental place than they were at the age of 20. The assumption that the mind deteriorates with age needs to be broken.

Sometimes, we move on to the next stage of being old, but we hang on to our experiences and habits of the past when our children were young and couldn't take care of themselves. An issue that bothers many parents is that they consider their grown-up married children as immature. This leads to excessive interference by parents in the marital life of their children. We have already spoken at length about this earlier.

This way, parents make themselves vulnerable to emotional abuse from not only their children but also the latter's spouses. Parents must restrain themselves so that children take their own decisions; and if they do happen to take wrong decisions, it will only help them become more mature. Stay away from the private life of your married children. Save your mental stability and your children's too.

If you have mental constructs that are impeding you from moving on and you keep thinking that life has been difficult, you must break some barriers and expand your horizon to see beyond them, as discussed in the previous chapters. In old age, problems of the mind can resonate more as we are not involved in creative, passionate work or physical work. It is common for older people to start suffering from fatigue, nausea, detachment from work and irritation. Sometimes, we do not recognize the stress that we have been carrying throughout our life, and this starts taking a toll. For example, it increases the production of acid in the gastrointestinal tract, induces frequent headaches, makes us lose our temper and causes nausea, anxiety and other psychosomatic symptoms. So, stay in touch with doctors and people your age who can help you.

Do something creative that has both a physical and mental component every day. Following is a list of hobbies that you can engage in:

- Astronomy
- Astrology
- Book clubs
- Computer classes
- Volunteering (NGO, community organization, etc.)
- Embroidery
- Painting

- Chess
- Crossword and other puzzles
- Jigsaw puzzles
- Creative writing: articles, poetry, books
- Dancing
- Photography
- Learning/playing a musical instrument
- Bird watching
- Gardening

Mental health is about intellectual growth, physical mobility and most importantly, the kind of food you eat. Small things may lead to big disasters or big changes in the quality of life. Let us make a promise to ourselves to reset our mind, body and spirit and overcome all conditioning and adversities to lead a healthy and wholesome life.

Acknowledgements

Many thanks to my grandparents, my wife—Pooja, my parents and my in-laws, who helped me in writing this book (my dear friend Prateek Madaan deserves a special mention here).

The book started against the backdrop of a lack of awareness about mental ailments in the prevalent social system. It is both educative and prescriptive and suggests various alternatives that will guide concerned individuals to take the right steps at the right time in order to both avoid and alleviate such ailments, should they occur.

Further, I am grateful to Shri Amar Singh Chandel, Pushpinder didi, Anup, Aman, Jeena, Aarzoo, Rakesh, Vaibhav, Rupali, Sushmita, Onkar, Somesh, Heramba Vigneshwar, Sourabh, Dr Hardeep Singh (Psychiatrist) and Dr Abhishek Saini (IAS), all of whom read this book and suggested amendments. I also extend my gratitude to friends, present and past, for their inspiration.

Lastly, I would like to acknowledge Dibakar Ghosh from Rupa Publications for believing in this book and for his able guidance every step of the way, and my editor Shatarupa Dhar, without whom the book would not be in the shape that it is today.

Glossary

Amygdala: Region in the brain primarily associated with emotional processes

Cerebral cortex: Outermost layer of our brain with a wrinkled appearance, also called grey matter

Cerebrospinal fluid: Colourless body fluid found within the tissue that surrounds the brain and spinal cord

Circadian rhythm: A 24-hour cycle that is a part of our body's internal clock; it regulates the sleep–wake cycle and other physical, mental, and behavioral changes

Cognitive: Relating to the mind, involving activities such as thinking, reasoning or remembering

Cortisol: Stress hormone

Dendrite: Short, branched extension of a nerve cell

Dopamine: Neurotransmitter that triggers feelings of pleasure, satisfaction and motivation

Endocannabinoids: Influences neuronal synaptic communication and affects biological functions, such as eating, anxiety, learning and memory, reproduction, metabolism, etc.

Endorphins: Hormones that relieve pain, reduce stress and improve our general sense of well-being

Ghrelin: Hormone produced by the stomach that sends signals to our brain when we are hungry

Glymphatic system: Recently discovered macroscopic waste clearance system in the brain

Hippocampus: Part of the brain that plays a major role in learning and memory

Hypothalamus: Part of the brain that controls body temperature, heart rate and hunger

Leptin: Hormone that sends a signal to the brain that inhibits hunger and influences the feeling of satiety

Limbic system: Group of subcortical structures (such as the hippocampus, hypothalamus and amygdala) in the brain that are usually concerned with emotion and motivation

Melatonin: Compound that helps with sleep by synchronizing the circadian rhythms

Morphine: A strong opiate that is mainly used as a pain medication

Neurons: Nerve cells

Neurotransmitters: Chemical messengers that transmit signals from one neuron (nerve cell) to the next neuron or a muscle cell.

Norepinephrine: Neurotransmitter that increases alertness, arousal levels and/or attention

Orbitofrontal cortex: Region in the brain involved in the cognitive process of decision-making; it is thought to represent emotion, taste, smell and reward

Opioid: Substances that act on opioid receptors to produce morphine-like effects

Oxytocin: Neurotransmitter that triggers feelings of love and protection

Paranoia: Mental illness wherein you wrongly believe that other people want to harm you

Parasympathetic nervous system: Part of the nervous system that relaxes the heart, dilates blood vessels, decreases pupil size, increases digestive juices and relaxes muscles in the gastrointestinal tract

Parkinson's disease: Neurological disorder that causes unintended or uncontrollable movements, such as shaking, stiffness and difficulty with balance and coordination

Pineal: Gland in the brain that secretes melatonin

Prefrontal cortex: Part of the brain that is highly developed in humans and plays a role in the regulation of complex cognitive and behavioural responses; it is also called the logical brain

Psychedelics: Class of psychoactive substances that bring about changes in perception, mood and cognitive processes; they affect all the senses, altering a person's thinking, sense of time and emotions.

Sympathetic nervous system: Nerves that help the body activate its 'fight-or-flight' response; it is activated when the body is stressed or in danger or physically active; it increases your heart rate and breathing, dilates your pupils and negatively affects processes like digestion

Synapses: Neuronal junction; the site of transmission of electric nerve impulses between two nerve cells

Toxoplasma gondii: Single-celled parasite that can infect most birds and animals, including humans

Vicodin: Drug prescribed as a pain reliever

Visceral nerve: Macroscopic cordlike structure, comprising a collection of nerve fibres that convey impulses between a part of the central nervous system and visceral organs